Welcome to Jerusalem: Adventures of a Newcomer

All rights reserved.

ISBN: 978-0-692-21588-3

Copyright © 5774/2014

Cover Design by: Chava Luque
Photography by: Channa Shapiro

"Your letters have given me a grand view of life in Israel."
Professor Herbert Ershkowitz

*"What a delight it is to read your letters.
Keeping up with the news doesn't give even a hint of what it's like on a personal level to enjoy Israeli life. We really love following your activities and feeling your enjoyment."*
Professor Emeritus Joseph Rubinstein, Purdue University

"You should compile your letters into a book."
Dr. Emily Taitz, Author

*"This book will be a nice gift for your children
and many generations to come."*
Heather Moskowitz, Lafayette, Indiana

"I have enjoyed reading the quotes from the Jerusalem Post conveyed with depth and breadth."
Dr. Elyakim Weisberg

*"Thanks so much for continuing to share
your interesting experiences with family and friends.
It brings back memories of my own experience in Israel."*
Dr. Lois Cohen, Sociologist

Welcome to Jerusalem: Adventures of a Newcomer

By: Cyrelle Simon

DEDICATION

This book is dedicated to my mother, Tania (Tova) Bernstein Ovsiew. My mother instilled in me, from an early age, an immense pride in being Jewish, combined with a Jewish education that included Hebrew, Yiddish, history, music and dancing. She enabled me to go on my first summer trip as a teenager to Israel with other group leaders and inculcated in me a firm attachment to the Jewish people and its land.

My second dedication is to my four children who have perpetuated my mother's values and, despite growing up in a small, Midwestern, primarily non-Jewish town, have grown to be scholars and rabbis who, with their spouses, now serve the Jewish people in Israel and abroad.

Last but not least, my third dedication is to my husband. Although his profession was biology professor, his studies and knowledge covered a large range of Jewish topics. He was a fervent supporter and defender of the State of Israel, visited very often, and worked here at Hadassah Hospital and the Weizmann Institute on his sabbaticals. He enabled me to fulfill my dream of making aliyah and living in the Holy Land.

Cyrelle Simon
Jerusalem
January 2014

ACKNOWLEDGMENTS

This book is a compilation of my "Letters from Jerusalem," which I have sent to my friends and family for five and a half years. The impetus for these letters was my desire to maintain contact with my former community in West Lafayette, Indiana, USA. Many of the letters were published in the Sons of Abraham Synagogue monthly bulletins. In addition, the recipients include family and friends far and wide. Readers' responses helped me reformulate some of my ideas, and their encouragement enabled me to create this volume.

I would like to thank my grandchildren Brocha Simon and Simcha Dovid Simon for helping with transcriptions. Simcha, as well as Yechiel Yaakov Comrov, Dovid Sholom Simon, Menachem and Nochum Dovid Pollack, and Yocheved Simon Wechsler have my gratitude for contributing information. I am appreciative of Yocheved's proofreading the manuscript and editing Chapter 6. Brocha also deserves my thanks for preparing and organizing the typesetting, the layout, and the cover.

My daughter Shira has encouraged me throughout my sending of these "Letters from Jerusalem," often asking pertinent questions regarding the contents. My son Rabbi Rashi deserves unending appreciation for never failing to respond to each letter throughout the five and a half years. His comments were often laudatory, with insightful information and occasional corrections. I eagerly looked forward to his evaluation of my epistles.

But most of all, I am indebted to my editor, Channa Shapiro, for her clarity of thinking, weeding out unnecessary phrases, restructuring sentences, and meticulously checking every fact. Channa ensured consistent literary technique throughout. She is most profusely thanked.

INTRODUCTION

A WORD ABOUT LANGUAGE

This book is written with numerous Hebrew and Yiddish words, as many of its readers are likely to appreciate this familiar terminology. A glossary of Hebrew and Yiddish terms, as well as basic Jewish concepts, can be found at the end. Please avail yourself of it liberally.

After my husband died in October 2006, Jerusalem became my home. We had lived over 45 years in a small, American Midwest college town, West Lafayette, Indiana. We arrived there in 1960 with a year-old infant when my husband, Edward, began his work as a biology professor at Purdue University. We then added two more children to the family. The fourth was born during one of our frequent sabbaticals in Israel.

As my children grew up, they left Lafayette. My eldest daughter, Shira, lives with her family in B'nei Brak, 30 miles from me. She is a birthing coach and is married to a Torah scholar. My son Rashi, living in London, is the rabbi of his own congregation, and his wife works with him in teaching and building the community. My younger son, Hillel, is assistant supervisor of kashrut for the London Beit Din. His wife is the Executive Vice President of International Development for the Kemach Foundation. Ronit, my youngest, works as a part-time kashrut supervisor and is married to a hospice rabbi in Milwaukee, Wisconsin. I am blessed to have 23 grandchildren at this date and 4 great-grandchildren. You will be introduced to some of them later in this work.

Throughout the years, we became very involved in that small Jewish community and made many close friends. My husband took leadership roles in several Jewish organizations, and I served in many volunteer positions, including president of the Sons of Abraham Sisterhood and the Lafayette Chapter of Hadassah. I also was privileged to work with a many young people in the Jewish community: leading Zionist youth groups as well as teaching pre-school, Hebrew classes, Sunday school, and private students.

For several years, I substitute taught in the local school system, and I also took great pleasure in teaching piano for over 15 years. I played the French horn in the Purdue Band, and participated in a recorder ensemble. In addition, I taught recorder and Israeli folk dance. I founded a number of Jewish communal activities, such as the Yiddish Club, the national award-winning Hadassah Study Group, and the musical ensemble Lafayette Klezmorim. I also established a cottage industry of baking and selling challot, hamantaschen, honey cakes, and other baked goods.

As the reader can see from my letters, the same interests I enjoyed in West Lafayette have permeated my life in Jerusalem: Jewish learning, Yiddish and Hebrew languages, piano and recorder playing.

Chapter 1

2008

January 2008

It's been six months since I began the Israeli chapter of my life and I'm still adjusting, learning new facts of daily living and viewing each experience with my American eyes.

Following a mountain of aliyah paper work, which was completed in the States, my flight and arrival last July was uneventful. A Nefesh B'Nefesh representative greeted me warmly and personally as I exited the plane with my 11-year-old grandson, Menachem. I was shepherded through customs, my luggage was quickly collected, and I was given a substantial sum of money from the government to help jumpstart my new life here. I also received my new *olah* document.

Nefesh B'Nefesh has many programs to help integrate newcomers, especially during their first year. A social worker calls monthly to help me solve problems, particularly bureaucratic ones.

Since my initial medical needs were urgent, I needed my daughter Shira, who has lived in Israel over 25 years, to help me navigate the healthcare system. While the actual care at the nearby clinic and Hadassah Hospital seems to be comparable to my U.S. experiences, I've had to learn a few facts, such as which papers to bring to which offices, getting used to waiting a long time for routine doctors' appointments, and most of all, taking the initiative for whatever issues and questions arise. I find the secretaries at the clinic and nurses at Hadassah Hospital to be particularly efficient, capable, and helpful.

My experience with dentists, on the other hand, is rather strange, or at least new. The two private dentists I've dealt with usually make their own appointments, and one even collects payment himself. Both spend time talking on the phone with personal calls while treating me. They also charge heavily, while disparaging the cheaper clinic dentists, so my private care is costing huge sums of money.

I'm still a novice in the area of banks, but I've learned that not only is no interest given on checking accounts, but there is a commission taken for every single service, even deposits, checks, and withdrawals. Converting dollars to shekel takes an impossible length of time, and there's usually no point at all in saving dollars in the bank. I locked away some dollars for three months and instead of earning, I lost money. The local money changers, however, offer good rates and do a brisk business. I prefer to use them whenever possible.

There is a stark contrast between my Happy Hollow cul-de-sac and my living room windows facing the main street in this neighborhood called Bayit VeGan, which means "House and Garden." In Lafayette, I could walk at least 15 minutes and not see a car or a person. The neighborhood was tree-lined, peaceful, and quiet. Here, the street is teeming with people, especially at 8:00 a.m. and 1:00 p.m. when the schoolchildren add to the din. Announcements, such as funerals, are made by a blaring loudspeaker on top of a car driving through the streets. Here, I know most of the storekeepers, who greet me personally and ask how I'm feeling and how I spent whatever holiday had just taken place.

Friday morning is an especially busy time in the neighborhood. One can feel, in people hurrying, the sense of the coming Shabbat. Also, certain offices are closed on Fridays, so more people are out and about. It is then that I have my weekly walk to the French bakery, the newspaper store, and the flower vendor. I pass and contribute to the few regular beggars asking for charity before Shabbat. When I give them *tzedakah*, they wish me good health and long life. My grandson Menachem tells me to take these *brachot* seriously, and he quotes a famous reference from the Talmud: "Do not take lightly a blessing by a simple person" [Tractate *Megillah* 15a].

By about 3:00 p.m., the street becomes quiet with the exception of some vehicular traffic. Fifteen minutes before candle lighting, loud and lively Jewish music resounds throughout the neighborhood. This is a signal to get ready to light. At the moment of candle lighting, a loud and long blast is sounded followed by utter quiet. About 15 minutes later, hordes of men appear on their way to shul. Women and children in their lovely clothes stroll in the streets and greet one another. One has to learn when to say "Gut Shabbos" and when to say "Shabbat Shalom." To Ashkenazic Chareidim, the greeting is "Gut Shabbos"; to Modern Orthodox, Sephardim, and *chilonim*, it's "Shabbat Shalom." About an hour and a half later, people begin to wend their way home as the men exit from shul.

Shabbat morning, again the streets are quiet and the shuls are full. Since some minyanim begin as early as 5:00 a.m. and others don't start until 9:30 a.m., *Kiddush* is recited and lunch is eaten at various times. Usually, the hours from 12:30-4:00 p.m. constitute rest time. Afterward, people emerge to partake of the many Shabbat classes available in the area, which are even offered in several languages. On Shabbat, the streets are completely closed to traffic, and it is fun to watch the fashion parade. Adults and children dress in their holiday finest; babies, covered with frilly blankets, lounge in their prams and strollers. There is, however, a car in the center of the neighborhood labeled "Shabbos Goy," which refers to a non-Jew who is available, in emergencies, to do certain tasks that a Jew may not do on Shabbat. There is also an Arab doctor in the nearby clinic.

Silence once again reigns in the streets as people eat *seudah shlishit*, the third Shabbat meal, eaten before sunset. The men then go to daven *Maariv* and return home a few minutes after Shabbat to make *Havdalah*.

The months since my aliyah in July have brought a number of holidays, and some of the public ways of celebrating here are interesting. The Egged buses, for example, displayed large signs: "Shanah Tovah" for Rosh HaShanah, "Gemar Chatimah Tovah" for Yom Kippur and "Chag Sameach" for Sukkot.

A few days before Yom Kippur, I found a crowd of kids on my street corner. They, accompanied by some mothers, were surrounding a large cage of chickens, which were being sold for *shlugging kaparos* – a custom in which you encircle your head three times with a chicken, or with money, and utter a prayer to ask forgiveness for your sins.

Immediately after Yom Kippur, with only four days until Sukkot, a nearby street was completely blocked to traffic. There was many a table, upon which sukkot decorations, *etrogim*, and *lulavim* were being displayed and sold. Vendors were doing a brisk business, and a colorful carnival atmosphere permeated the scene.

Before Tu B'Shvat, luscious produce was available, particularly fruits typical of the holiday, such as figs, dates, almonds, and others. The custom on Tu B'Shvat is to eat fruits from the seven species for which the Land of Israel is praised: "It is a land of wheat, barley, (grape) vines, figs, and pomegranates; a land of oil-olives and (date) honey" [Deut. 8:8].

Some people, however, eat 15 fruits of Israel, corresponding to the date, 15th Shvat. Others eat at least 29 different fruits on the holiday. My granddaughter and her husband follow this custom. Many conduct a fruit-filled Tu B'Shvat seder! This year, probably more than usual, fruit is imported because it is the *shmitah* year when the fields lie fallow, and there are various laws pertaining to when and how certain produce can be grown.

Sunday, February 10, 2008

My children treated me to a long-wished-for vacation at a hotel by the Dead Sea. The Golden Tulip Hotel, at the foot of the sea, features plentiful, delicious, and varied food as well as clean and tidy premises. But best of all is the opportunity to soak in the Dead Sea pool, sulfur pool, and jacuzzi, and to enjoy the wet and dry saunas, mud baths, massages, and more. I reveled in the exercise classes, calming air, and general pampering. There is also convenient access to the sea itself. At dusk, one beholds the mauve colored mountains of Moav, today's Jordan. At night we were offered slapstick entertainment, dancing, quizzes, and group singing usually accompanied by loud rhythmic music. I was amused to learn that the gym was called *cheder kosher*, the fitness room. The bus trip each way provided a chance to enjoy the striking desert mountain scenery.

Back in Jerusalem, the advent of snow provided one of my startling experiences. The expected foot of wet snow was the subject of the media and conversations for days. When it finally arrived, buses were rented in B'nei Brak to bring people up to Jerusalem. In addition, the mayor, Rabbi Uri Lupoliansky, sent two truckloads of snow to B'nei Brak for those who couldn't make the trip. The sidewalks here, covered with snow, were very slippery. People tied plastic bags around their shoes to protect them, and when the snow receded a day later, brown plastic bags adorned the sidewalks. The streets were the safest place to walk because traffic had, in good part, melted the snow. When I queried the storekeepers as to why they didn't purchase snow shovels, the response was, "What, for once a year?" Actually, there was a second brief snowfall a few weeks later. The city, of course, completely shut down, there was no school, and many events were canceled. I had a ticket for a major Irish Dance performance in one of Jerusalem's largest halls. The dance troupe, numbering close to several hundred, remained here another few days and the event was rescheduled.

Monday, March 10, 2008

All of Israel was horrified and saddened by last Thursday night's shooting of eight yeshiva boys who were studying at Mercaz Harav, founded by first Chief Rabbi of Israel Avraham Yitzchak HaCohen Kook and located at the entrance of Jerusalem. In this yeshiva, students are imbued with love for Torah and love for the Land of Israel. I know the father of one of the martyrs and remember his grandparents and great-grandparents. He was from such a warm, fine, bright, giving family. May each boy's memory be for a blessing.

On a happy note, last night my upstairs neighbors, who are warm and generous people, hosted a *l'chayim*—a swift, impromptu celebration of an engagement—for their 12th of 14 children. Each married child brought something, and on a half day's notice there was loads of food to offer the hundreds of people who came to celebrate. It was a joyous occasion.

In these arranged marriages, the boy and girl generally meet only a few times, checking in with the *shadchan* (professional matchmaker) after each date if they want to continue meeting. They usually decide on the fourth date or so, and if they plan to marry, the *l'chayim* takes place immediately. I would add that *shadchanim* demand high fees here – in the thousands of dollars. Some *shadchanim* only work for the children of rebbes and rebbitzens. That specialty commands greater recompense.

I'm invited each Shabbat for every meal so I get to know many people fairly well. On one occasion, I lost my eyeglasses while walking home on Friday night. Despite some effort, they weren't found. A friend told me of a neighborhood lost-and-found bulletin board centrally located. She helpfully pinned a notice on the board describing my loss. I had a phone response about a week later – wrong glasses. Some weeks after that, a caller said he had found my glasses and noticed the note on the bulletin board. He brought them to me, saying he was happy to do the mitzvah of returning lost items.

Sunday, March 30, 2008

Purim has been in the air from the advent of the first month of Adar, and discussion and plans intensified in this leap year's second Adar. I had been excitedly anticipating Jerusalem's three-day Purim when each of the four mitzvot is allocated to a specific day. On Shabbat, certain readings and prayers were added while others were eliminated. Taanit Esther was on Thursday, and the *Megillah* was read on Thursday night and Friday morning. *Matanot l'evyonim* was on Friday, and the special meal and *mishloach manot* delivery are both today, Sunday. I sent about 15 quite elaborate parcels, which were delivered by my daughter Shira and her 11-year-old son, Shmuel, who visited for the day. I received very creative and interesting parcels in return. Several stores in the neighborhood had a Purim *shuk*, a mini-market featuring all the supplies one would need in preparing *mishloach manot*, such as paper, baskets, and ribbons. These shops also offered—besides the usual *mon* (poppy seed) hamantaschen—the following array for variety: chocolate, rosemary, nuts, halvah, whole wheat, dates, and sugarless. I haven't seen any apricot-filled, which was one of my specialties. My grandson, 18-year-old Menachem, brought eight yeshiva boys to my home for the Purim *seudah* and they drank, ate, sang, and danced for many hours. It was a time of much revelry and merriment. There were a lot of noisy firecrackers in the street to add to the excitement.

During this month, I attended three weddings, a *brit*, a bat mitzvah, and an evening of *Sheva Brachot*. Weddings here are noisy, obstreperous, and full of children of all ages dressed in their finery. Chuppot are held outside. A small wedding may consist of 60 or 70 people, but I've only been to one such affair. Most weddings include hundreds of guests who are served a full-course meal with plenty of extras. The seating at Chareidi affairs is separate, and at all religious weddings, dancers are separated by a *mechitza*. The music is usually loud.

I was recently invited to an Amen party. I was interested in learning about this type of gathering, begun only a few years ago as a women's Jewish-spiritual ritual. The hostess describes the proceedings. She serves various foods that require different *brachot*, and each *bracha* has its own virtue: the blessing on fruit of the tree, for children; the blessing on fruit of the vine, for finding a marriage partner; blessings on other food, for livelihood. She asks one person to say a particular *bracha* – for example, *borei pri ha'etz* on an apple. The person making the *bracha* can add a relevant comment, such as "This *bracha* should be for good *parnassa*." Everyone in attendance responds with "Amen." The more people, the greater power "Amen" has in heaven.

I learned something very interesting not long ago. My friend's granddaughter married a Belzer Chassid. Chassidim are known to have *payot* (sidelocks), and different dynasties sport different styles. Some have long, twisted locks that hang down on each side of the face; others curl one behind each ear. This man had hair, but not enough to grow the lovely ringlets. So, I found out that a man can buy *payot* and affix them in some way to the head, since this item is an integral part of a Belzer Chassid's appearance.

Monday, April 28, 2008

Beginning in November, advertisements abound in the newspapers for hotels and resorts for Pesach, and the intensity increases as the holiday draws near. Also, new clothes and kitchen utensils are purchased. On almost each street block, the week before Pesach, I saw large vats billowing steam. People were coming to *kasher* their utensils. The older children begin their vacation two weeks before Pesach so they can help prepare for the big event. Many people here do not eat prepared food on the holiday, so impromptu vegetable stands are set up on the street.

When I taught in the shul nursery school and the temple Sunday preschool, I remember reading a pre-Pesach book entitled *Everything's Changing*. For me, this Pesach was a different take on that theme. No cleaning, no searching for *chametz*, no special shopping or asking all my friends to bring particular items from Chicago, no covering the counters, no inviting guests, and so forth. A bit apprehensively, I joined Shira and six of her seven children for a gratifying week at Kibbutz Chafetz Chayim's guest houses. The atmosphere; the very pastoral scene of green lawns and bright flowers; pleasant weather; delicious, varied, fresh, and plentiful food; and the high-level, inspirational programs for the entire family made the week a gastronomic and spiritual delight. An added treat was the opportunity to bond with Shira and her family. I did sing my late husband Ed's tunes to myself during the seder, which my son-in-law Shlomo conducted in the big dining room that housed about 20 sedarim at once.

Monday, May 26, 2008

Yom HaShoah and Yom HaZikaron were often in the news at the end of last month and early in May. They are sad occasions. I attended four programs commemorating the Holocaust, including two at Yad Vashem and one in which Mike Blain, long-time Israel Bonds Chair of Indiana, spoke at a women's college about his wartime experiences. Another moving ceremony took place at Yad Vashem on Yom HaZikaron, and again thousands of people attended. The ceremonies were very poignant, including sad music, prayers, and speeches by the president, prime minister, and of course the chief rabbis.

A weather pattern typical of the Middle East is the *sharav*, or *chamsin*. The Hebrew word *sharav* is found in Isaiah 35:7 and 49:10 where it means "dry heat." According to Arab tradition, a *chamsin*, the Arabic word for 50, is most likely to occur during the 50 days between Easter and Pentecost. The *chamsin's* hot, dry winds from North Africa blow over Israel, bringing sand from the desert. I, who rarely have headaches, was affected by the oppressively hot *sharav* with a typical headache. For relief, one should drink copious amounts of water.

At a recent Shabbat dinner I learned that although there are an enormous variety of *Kiddush* cups available here, there are some that are more appropriate for different groups of people. My host explained that his custom was to use one without a stem and with an uncurved rim, and he gave Talmudic sources to substantiate his choice. Besides the shape of a *Kiddush* cup, size is also a factor. People differ in their requirements for the cup dimensions. My son-in-law follows the ruling of the Chazon Ish, a 20th-century sage, who recommended the largest size. Since it is halachically preferable for the person making *Kiddush* to drink a bit over half the cup, most people to whom I've been invited drink only grape juice.

Last Thursday night was Lag BaOmer, which is a major celebration here. *Medurot* are, of course, in every vacant spot. Over one quarter of a million people go to Mount Meron to see the main bonfire lit by the Boyaner Rebbe whose ancestor, Rabbi Yisrael of Ruzhin, many years ago purchased the right to light this fire on the roof of the tomb of Rabbi Shimon Bar Yochai. However, my grandson Menachem, who traveled there last year, said the traffic jams were horrendous—as much as a seven-hour trip each way—and he quipped, "It's easier to eat than to pray in Meron." Many charitable groups vie for the honor of feeding the visitors; however, access to the actual cave of Shimon Bar Yochai is just about impossible.

I want to mention that the produce here is especially tasty. Although this is a *shmitah* year, making the prices higher than usual, I find that produce is one of the least expensive food items. Whereas in the States all produce is available throughout the year, in Israel many items can be found only when they are in season. For me, it is also a delight to enjoy many yoghurt-type foods as well as the big variety of *hummus*, *techina*, and *chatzilim* (eggplant) dips available.

WEDNESDAY, JUNE 11, 2008

Last week, I enjoyed several major events. The first treat began on Erev Yom Yerushalayim when I participated in a lovely bar mitzvah party. The outstanding venue was a *tayelet* (promenade) located at the southeastern end of Jerusalem from which one can see an astonishing view of the city. Chairs were set up on a veranda, and a *chazan* chanted a very special service for Yom Yerushalayim. It was a breathtaking and uplifting experience. The bar mitzvah boy gave an impressive *drasha*, and the food, music, and ambiance were delightful.

Another of last week's special events was a private tour of the Weizmann Institute in Rechovot. Hearing some reports from scientists was enlightening. In particular, my friend and I learned of the work of Prof. J. Stevens, a physicist who explores "the consequences of damage and genome variation in various biological contexts by manipulating single molecules using new-fangled physical techniques and by following biological processes in single cells." We met some Lafayette friends for lunch in the Weizmann Cafe.

The farthest I traveled that week was to Eilat. There is a plethora of beautiful hotels, which is obviously good for the economy, and I was comfortably ensconced in Le Méridien. Besides the unending beauty and majesty of the desert, viewed on my trip from Jerusalem to Eilat and back, there was the marvelous oceanarium. The underwater fish observatory is a really unusual experience and, with an English audio guide, I was able to learn something about the many rare and beautiful creatures. The site is actually a small park and houses a building of uncommon fish peculiar to the area. I'm eager to return for a longer visit.

Finally, to top off the week, I went to Tel Aviv with my friend Fred Blank, had a delicious, kosher Argentinean steak for lunch, and then bought a Yamaha upright piano. It's not the same quality as my West Lafayette Grand, but it does come close. I have had a nice piano practically since I've been here, but the quality has been fair; still, I've been able to sell it.

Shavuot, this week, was a pleasant family experience. I spent the holiday in B'nei Brak, my first time ever celebrating only one day. My great-grandson and his parents were at Shira's home, along with the rest of the family. Food was delicious and plentiful. I made it up the four or five flights of stairs to the women's section of the shul.

Wednesday, July 2, 2008

Today, an Arab resident of East Jerusalem used a bulldozer to attack several cars in the center of the city, killing 3 people and wounding at least 30 pedestrians. It's a sad day.

On a happier note, recently I've been invited to four weddings in four weeks. And in the year that I've been living here, I've been to at least six weddings. This has reminded me about the short space of time that Ashkenazim alot for weddings. It occurred to me that during my first eight years in Lafayette, there were no shul weddings at all. The period between Shavuot and The Three Weeks is the shortest time span of the year in which Ashkenazim celebrate weddings. I learned some of the customs recently. Apparently, weddings are rarely performed during the month of Tishrei, at least throughout the holiday season. And while Chareidi yeshivot discourage weddings during the month of Elul, Chassidim actively encourage these celebrations during that month. They each cite their own sources.

My community is a safe one. It is not unusual to see a 5-year-old child leading a younger sibling, perhaps 3 years old, by the hand. When the pair needs to cross the street, they will wait at a designated area until any adult passes who wants to cross at the same spot. The adults know to invite the children to join them. I've experienced this encounter a number of times.

I have lived in 17 rented apartments in Bayit VeGan. The current one, which I own, is my first to have an elevator. After almost a year, I still find it amazing that there is a mezuzah at the elevator door.

Within the last two weeks, I've had several fascinating visits to museums. One was a meaningful and educational trip to Beit Hatfutsot, the Diaspora Museum; another was to the new Palmach Museum. Both of these are in Tel Aviv. In addition, I spent a most enlightening day in Zichron Yaakov where

I saw the Beit Aharonson Museum, as well as a museum featuring the First Aliyah, which began in 1882 and lasted until 1903. I also toured the Carmel Winery, which was founded there by Baron Edmond de Rothschild in 1892, one year after he established the Carmel Winery in Rishon LeTzion. I found all the museums and tours to be very well planned, utilizing effective technology.

Last week, I enjoyed a rare Jerusalem event. When you come into the city, at the very entrance you'll see a massive string bridge called Gesher HaMeitarim (The Jerusalem Chords Bridge). This is planned to eventually expedite the Jerusalem Light Rail, or tramway, in the hope of solving some of the city's heavy traffic problems, soon and for years to come. The bridge is said to symbolize King David's harp. I was given a ticket to the dedication ceremony, which was attended by many thousands of people and included fireworks, acrobats, singers, musicians, and some appropriate speeches given by dignitaries. It was entertaining and moving – an unusual experience.

I learned a Hebrew slang expression recently. First, some background. It's common for elderly or infirm people to employ a private live-in aide, and they are generally from the Philippines – a female Philippinit, or a man would be a Philippino. An acquaintance of mine said her mother has a good Ukrainian Philippinit. Mystified, I queried, "How could that be?" I then realized that Philippinit has become a generic term for a live-in helper or caretaker.

Jerusalem's summer weather is idyllic. However, I must add the fact that from 11:00 a.m. to 4:00 p.m. I have the luxury of remaining in my air-conditioned apartment. Perspiration evaporates immediately in the dry heat, and I never use my clothes dryer since the laundry dries swiftly when I hang it on my porch line. Evenings are cool and breezy, so I always take a stole or sweater when I go out at night.

I enjoyed a delightful dinner with friends at Moshav Ora. The café was in a plant nursery, a very attractive setting. It is about 15 minutes from Jerusalem and is the site of many Chareidi weddings. Ashkenazic Chareidi Jews have the custom of not using musical instruments at a wedding or similar *simcha* in Jerusalem proper, in remembrance of the destruction of the *Beit HaMikdash*. This proscription does not include singers or percussion players. So, if the family should like to use musical instruments, certain areas that were not in ancient Jerusalem are popular wedding locales.

Monday, July 14, 2008

One aspect of my good fortune in living here is the fact that I have warm and generous neighbors. Across the hall is a young couple with four boys aged 2 to 7. They are living with friends for three weeks while their apartment is rented out to another family. This is a very common way for young people to earn some extra money in the summer. They rent their apartment to people from other parts of the country and crowd into their parents' home for a few weeks. There is also a couple, recently arrived from France, who are part of a huge influx of French Jews who began moving here several years ago and have driven up apartment prices in the neighborhood. Last but not least, my upstairs neighbors are such a warm, close, and generous family. They have 14 children, 12 of whom are married. I attended the weddings of two of their offspring recently and was invited to *Sheva Brachot* parties, which were very festive events. There are untold numbers of grandchildren. To my delight, I learned that two daughters-in-law are from my home state, New Jersey, and went to the same high school that my daughter Shira attended in Elizabeth.

Today, I went to a *brit* celebrated by this family in a lovely hotel. All the children and their spouses attend almost every family event. Last night we had the *vach nacht*, when 10 of the male grandchildren came and stood around the newborn's bassinet saying the Shema, Adon Olam, and several other prayers. Each youngster received a bag of treats. It was fun!

My friend and piano partner has 9 children, about 70 grandchildren, and at least 17 great-grandchildren. Their numbers are typical for Chareidi families. People generally marry young, and there is now a major housing shortage despite the constant construction in many areas. My friend and her husband made aliyah from the States about 40 years ago. She teaches piano, and her husband has a Ph.D. in chemistry and a law degree from Columbia University. He's held a number of government positions including Assistant Minister of Science for the State of Israel.

Although I don't have data, I think the combined religious populations are a minority in the State of Israel. However, *The Jerusalem Post* quoted a government source saying that Chareidim make up a third of the Jerusalem population and 48 percent of the city's school children.

I recently enjoyed two performances, by famous Yiddish singer Dudu Fisher and by a very talented klezmer back-up group. The 950-seat Jerusalem

Theater was sold out for both events.

When acquaintances or friends meet or greet on the phone, the repartee will often be the following: "Mah nishmah?" (What's up?), "Mah chadash?" (What's new?), "Mah ha'inyanim?" (What's of interest?), and sometimes "Mah shlomeich?" (How are you?) will be asked. The most common response, mainly by religious but often secular people as well, is *"Baruch Hashem."* I sometimes think that such a response helps people to focus on the fact that everything is essentially G-d ordained, and they can accept whatever Hashem accords them.

Since Israel is so small, I learned of another area in which Israelis tend to know or be related to one another. In the past, when a policeman stopped a speeding car and he and the driver began to converse, they invariably discovered they had a mutual friend, had attended the same school, or were distantly related, so drivers were rarely ticketed. That was when the government decided to use radar to track cars, since it is a more effective way to fine speeders.

Getting married is vital among Orthodox Jews, and to this end I attended a meeting in my neighborhood this evening. About 14 women were present, and each one suggested a person who was looking for a match. Of course, many more women than men are available, but it was an inspiring event with people taking notes and trying to help singles aged 19 to 45 find their *bashert*. The meeting was serious but pleasant, taking place in a home with a comfortable atmosphere.

WEDNESDAY, JULY 23, 2008

A second bulldozer attack took place here yesterday. Given the fact that there were many wounded and in shock, it is miraculous that there were no deaths. The assailant was killed by a former army officer who is actually a farmer. Because of the *shmitah* year, the farmer wasn't working on the land. Instead, he is doing odd jobs and happened to be on King David Street witnessing the attack. He lives in a small village called Sussya, which is actually an ancient archaeological site as well. Since the village is isolated, he is permitted to carry a gun and was able to use it to prevent another horrific tragedy such as the one that happened three weeks ago.

I recently enjoyed a four-day trip to Kibbutz Lavi in the Galilee. Highlights included lectures in Jewish History by the talented Rabbi Berel

Wein, a visit to one of three shofar makers in Israel, and a visit to Moshav Kinneret, home of the famous poetess Rachel, whose verses were put to well-known songs such as "Kinneret Sheli" and "Sham Harei Golan." The shofar maker showed us antlers from various kinds of animals, including the ibex, oryx, and others. The only impermissible antlers are from the bull, because of the Jewish people's sin with the Golden Calf. We also visited the only winery that produces wine from pomegranates, and the Hula Valley in which birds migrating from Europe to Africa take a rest stop. Our group picnicked in a grove of Eucalyptus trees. ("Chorshat HaEucalyptus" was one of the very lovely songs the Lafayette Klezmorim often performed.)

Sunday, August 24, 2008

My summer was fortunately filled with visits from my son Rashi and his family; two of Hillel and Yael's children, who visited briefly; Ronit and her daughter Rivka, who vacationed here; and finally, Shira, Shlomo, and six of their seven children. They all reveled in the Jerusalem weather and in the educational and spiritual offerings. What was quite a new experience to me was the fact that Shira's 9-year-old daughter frequently went to the grocery for me. She bought the items on my list, and returned with them and the correct change.

Somewhat shocking to my American sensibilities is learning about discrimination by some Ashkenazic schools towards Sephardim. According to a friend, these schools have a quota of 30 percent Sephardic students. I don't know if the situation is reversed in Sephardic schools.

My knowledge in the area of Chareidi children's education is very scanty. However, what is of interest to me on a superficial level is the fact that Chareidi kids are in separate classes from around age 3 and above. The girls do learn some English from fourth through eighth grades, and they also learn some secular subjects through high school. The boys never learn English, and from about seventh grade on, they study Talmud (Mishnah and Gemara) and many other religious subjects.

However, at home my daughter Shira has done an outstanding job of teaching English— speaking, reading, and writing—to all of her children. This, given the fact that the kids speak Hebrew to one another, and that Shira speaks Hebrew to her husband, Shlomo, is an impressive feat.

She is especially delighted that her daughter Tovah is speaking only

English to her children.

My granddaughter Tovah lives in Kiryat Sefer, the only all-Chareidi city in all of Israel. Entry into this city is carefully selected, and no apartment can be bought by a non-Chareidi family. Most often, men sit and learn Torah for their whole lives. On Tovah's block there are five shuls: Yemenite, Sephardic, and Chassidic, bounded by one Ashkenazic on either side. Tovah's husband, Shauli, walks about 15 minutes to the only shul where the davening is according to the German *minhag* of Anshel Mayer Rothschild. Besides being the nephew of Jerusalem Mayor Rabbi Lupolianski, Shauli is a direct descendant of the famous Shimshon Raphael Hirsch of Frankfurt.

At one of my Shabbat invitations, I complimented the host on his melodic singing of the Shabbat melodies. He responded that he and his brother are Levites, and one of the tasks of the Levites in the ancient Temple in Jerusalem was chanting during the services. He and his family are preparing to officiate at the building of the Third Temple, may it be speedily in our day.

Monday, September 22, 2008

The word *gemach* is an abbreviation of *gemilut chassadim* (acts of kindness). We had such a group in Lafayette for many years. By paying a yearly fee, members could borrow money without interest so long as they had a co-signer. Decisions were made by a small committee of senior members. Once a year, we all held a business meeting and ate a tasty hot dog supper.

Israeli *gemachim* abound. My Chareidi phone book lists about 2,500 *gemachim* for religious families in Jerusalem and the surrounding area. There are no membership fees as in Lafayette, and most items are for borrowing and returning. Sometimes, a small donation is expected. A random sample includes low chairs for sitting shivah; all kinds of religious books for study; bridal gowns that must be cleaned before returning; feather quilts for brides to keep; dishes for special occasions; and fancy chocolates, such as in the shape of *tefillin* for a bar mitzvah celebration.

My friend, who was recently widowed, was able to get free, beautiful new clothes for Rosh HaShanah and some winter coats for her three young children. There are amulets to put over the bed of a woman giving birth, maternity clothes, Shabbat candles, inhalers, and on and on. It is truly amazing what a self-help society this is, and the biblical injunction to take care of the poor, the needy, the widow, and the orphan is heeded here.

Wednesday, October 22, 2008

My family and I just commemorated my husband Ed's second *yahrtzeit*. My sons, Rashi and Hillel, came here from London and there were 14 family members at the gravesite. We all recited certain verses from *Tehillim*, chosen for each one of the letters in Ed's Hebrew name, and my sons contributed short remarks. He is buried on a mountain with a striking, beautiful panoramic view of Jerusalem.

Tuesday, December 2, 2008

Everyone in Israel was terribly upset by the recent tragedies in India, and it was such a sad day here when the Chabad rabbi and his wife were buried in Har Hazeitim… lots of traffic jams in Jerusalem on Tuesday.

On a happier note, I've recently returned to Jerusalem from a *nachesdig* trip to Milwaukee and London. In Milwaukee we celebrated the birth of Nechama Leba Miriam, whose parents are Ronit (Simon) and Boruch Comrov. The baby's big brother, Menachem, started putting on *tefillin*. He was taught personally by Rabbi Twerski who officiated at the ritual, which is traditionally begun at least a month before a boy's bar mitzvah. We sponsored a *Kiddush* at the shul on Shabbat where the baby was named, and then brought some light refreshments the next day to celebrate Menachem's special occasion. Shortly after, in London we celebrated the grand bar mitzvah of Hillel's son Levi, who is very talented and learned the entire *parshah* and *haftarah*. Levi was the first bar mitzvah to *lein* from the Torah that my family and friends dedicated in Ed's memory. Services were held in a private home rather than in a shul.

Back home in Bayit VeGan, there are many shuls within several blocks of my apartment, each with a different focus or tradition. If you were walking down the street, it would not be unusual to see tens of men outside davening together, forming impromptu outdoor minyanim. From my porch I can hear the music of a nearby Chassidic shul called Sochatchov. Since the neighborhood was originally planned for schools, there is a wide variety of educational institutions, and at certain times of the day the area is filled with youngsters of all ages.

As always, I'm interested in language. Words that have entered the vocabulary in Israel include: "le-condel," named after former United States

Secretary of State Condoleezza Rice, who visited here often – the term means to be busy with meetings and accomplish nothing; "le-hizdangeff," named after Dizengoff Street in Tel Aviv, means to stroll leisurely and window shop. You may have read about the new Israeli two-shekel coin called the "shnekel," combining the words shnei shekel, two shekel.

Wednesday, December 31, 2008

Chanukah is festive here, as everywhere. Some particular scenes include a very large table in my neighborhood set out on the sidewalk displaying every kind of *chanukiyah*; large bottles of olive oil - which many people here use - with the warning "Not fit for consumption"; candles, often large so that they will be sure to burn the required half hour after dark; *ptilim* (wicks); and other relevant items. Since the command is to publicize the *neis* (miracle), in addition to the myriad *chanukiyot* visible in every window, near the outside doors to the buildings are large, rectangular, glass boxes in which are enclosed oil menorahs burning merrily. The religious girls have no school for most of Chanukah, but the boys only have three days vacation. Trips and visits are de rigueur for this season, and I have my very own family, Rashi's eldest daughter, Yocheved, spending her vacation here with me. I'm also looking forward to welcoming former students from Lafayette, who will be visiting for a few days after their tour has ended.

I celebrated the eighth and last day—called *Zot Chanukah*, from the verse read on this day at shul—at my daughter Shira's family gathering in B'nei Brak and casually asked her two older sons what they did during their brief vacation. Menachem, the elder one, said he made latkes, which I soon sampled, enjoying their tastiness and amazingly precise circular forms. The 17-year-old, Mordechai, said he was working, grinding grains by hand, to make matzah flour. And so, I learned what *matzah mehudar* is. Pesach matzah is made from flour kept dry from the time it is ground until it is baked in less than 18 minutes. For *shmurah matzah* (literally, "guarded matzah"), the wheat is watched from the time it is harvested so that no moisture affects it. It is considered a further beautification of the mitzvah, making it more expensive as well, if matzah is made from flour that has been hand ground, which is what my grandson was preparing. Handmade *shmurah matzah* is round, while machine-made *shmurah* matzah is *square*. Interesting, isn't it?

Chapter 2

2009

Tuesday, January 6, 2009

Today, the 10th of Tevet, commemorates the breaching of the walls of the First Temple. I learned that it is also the day when *Kaddish* is said for all the people who died in the Shoah. Because Yom HaShoah falls in the month of Nissan, when it is not appropriate to mourn or say eulogies, the rabbis have decreed that today, in every shul, *Kaddish* is said for all those Holocaust victims who lost their lives and whose graves and dates are unknown.

Because we are a small, caring country, the fighting in the Gaza Strip has reverberated everywhere. In B'nei Brak, my daughter Shira's children's school has taken in "refugees" from Ashdod as all schools there, along with the rest of the South, canceled their classes. Some children are learning in their shelters as the teachers are televising the lessons. All over the country people are saying *tehillim* for the safety of the soldiers. The universities have promised that the soldiers, upon their return, will be aided to make up missed work. I live about one mile from the military cemetery where five soldiers were interred today, one after the other. There are many organizations that are mobilizing to help all the people in the targeted areas.

Despite the grim situation, this war has the support of a large majority of Israelis who couldn't allow the untenable situation in Sderot to continue. The city has been hit by Kassam rockets for eight years. We hope and pray that this war will end victoriously and soon.

When the war ceased, I had the opportunity to enjoy five days at Kibbutz Ein Gedi which is situated less than two miles from the Ein Gedi Dead Sea Spa. The kibbutz has a fascinating ancient history. It is on the biblical site of the same name, and continuous Jewish settlement has existed there for more than 1,300 years. When David was pursued by King Saul, he hid in the Ein Gedi area. The villagers in those days made their living from growing the famous *afarsimon* and producing its perfume. Further evidence of Ein Gedi's fragrant vineyards can be found in Song of Songs [1:14]: "My beloved is unto me as a cluster of henna in the vineyards of Ein Gedi." I was told that the site is an archaeologist's Disneyland.

The modern kibbutz, which was established in 1956, was founded by members of a youth movement who later served in the Nachal unit of the army. They planted an astonishing variety of trees, grass, flowers and plants. There are now more than 900 species of vegetation from all over the world growing there. Primarily, there are date and ornamental palms as well as flora, which are unique to this internationally known Botanical Garden. Also, more than 1,000 species of cactus and unusual trees that produce myrrh and frankincense flourish in this unusual site. By the way, it is the only such garden in which people dwell.

As you know, the Dead Sea is the lowest and most salty lake in the world with a wealth of minerals. I was told it produces the greatest income of any venture in Israel. I personally reveled in the therapeutic mud, which possesses some of the highest concentration of medically beneficial minerals to be found anywhere. I also dipped in the sulphur pool and the very invigorating sulphur showers. The oxygen and bromide-rich air made me feel very calm, and I read that the higher air density lowers blood pressure. For me, the fun part consisted of doing yoga, Pilates (first time ever), and of course exercises and swimming in the spacious and almost empty kibbutz pool.

This was a group sponsored program, so I traveled by car with some friends and met other friends once we arrived. Because the group was Chareidi and needed a particular *hechsher*, special *mashgichim* were imported, one from as far as Tzfat. The food was plentiful, healthful and delicious. You can see that this was a really refreshing experience for me. As befits a Chareidi group, we didn't go mixed swimming, so the various pools were either duplicated, or had special hours for men and women only. Even the Dead Sea beach was dedicated for use by either women or men only.

A final note on this visit is that one night's entertainment at the kibbutz consisted of a talented Russian klezmer trio. Much to my delight, I knew every song and *freilach* they played and felt proud of our own Lafayette Klezmorim's repertoire. Our group played almost every number that these musicians knew, including lots of Yiddish songs and a very few from *Fiddler on the Roof*.

When I recently took a taxi from Jerusalem to B'nei Brak, I chatted with my Yemenite driver. He related a few interesting anecdotes. His parents were engaged in Yemen when they were 8 and 9 years old, although he added that they didn't live together then. Several years later, in 1929, both families made aliyah to Jerusalem with a number of other Yemenite families. At the ages of 13 and 14, the pair was married in Jerusalem. On another subject he said that his father can read Hebrew upside down, as he spread a book on the kitchen table and taught his children while sitting opposite them. He also said that all Yemenite boys rehearse every weekly *parshah* at home. They must be prepared when they go to shul, as the *gabbai* points to someone for each *aliyah la-Torah*, and the designated man or boy needs to be ready to lead the chanting. It is an insult to have a *baal korei* (official Torah reader) *lein* for him. He also reminded me that just as most Sephardim do, Yemenites chant all of *Shir HaShirim* (Song of Songs) each Friday night in shul.

The next day, while I was talking to a friend, she stated in some context that her Moroccan daughter-in-law was one of 17 children. And, therein lies a tale. The girl's father was 18 when he was engaged to a 3-year-old girl, her mother. Since he would have to wait a while to marry her, he was permitted to take another wife for about 10 years, but when the 3-year-old became of age, he had to divorce the first wife and marry his first fiancée. He sired a son with the first wife and had 17 children with his second.

I attended a *brit* in an amazing shul. It's called Belz and is situated at one of the highest points in Jerusalem. It is also very beautiful. The first rebbe of Belz took great interest in the construction of his beautiful shul, dedicated in 1843, and he was familiar with every detail. It was ordered destroyed by the Nazis in 1939, but an enlarged replica was erected in Jerusalem. Like the original shul, the Belz Great Synagogue also took 15 years to complete, and it was dedicated in 2000. I was told that according to halachah a shul should be higher than the surrounding buildings, and this one certainly is. The whole area is called Kiryat Belz, and, as you can imagine, abounds with Chassidim.

Wednesday, February 4, 2009

Tu B'Shvat and elections are in the air. I have been invited to two Tu B'Shvat sedarim and am looking forward to both events. One invite is from Cyril and Shirley Domb. Cyril is a famous physicist who taught at Bar-Ilan University for many years and previously at Oxford, England. He edited a well-known book called *Challenge* in which my husband Ed published an article entitled "Gene Creation." It deals with the Jewish and scientific views of evolution.

Few people here live in private homes, which are called villas, and apartment buildings are often quite close to one another. In my former small apartment, without a dryer, my husband was in charge of hanging the laundry on the porch line, which he did very skillfully. On Shabbat a friend invited me to visit an elderly relative of hers who lived nearby. Imagine my amazement when this former neighbor said, "I knew your husband," and then proceeded to show me the vista from her apartment where she could very clearly see my former porch line and view Ed hanging out the laundry! I was really surprised. By the way, I found out that this lady was in Chevron in 1929 when there was a terrible pogrom. Her father, who was a baker there, was killed and her mother lost a finger. The mother and her large family were, of course, forced to leave.

I met a friend at the Eretz Israel Museum, in Tel Aviv, and we enjoyed an interesting exhibit featuring James de Rothschild from France, who generously financed the early settlers of modern Israel. There was also an outstanding pottery exhibit of very talented and imaginative Israeli craftsmen.

I spent a Shabbat recently with Shira's family in B'nei Brak. As I was walking to the bus, about 45 minutes after Shabbat ended, I noticed that the traffic lights were not working. My grandson Shmuel, who accompanied me, reminded me that the city shuts off the traffic lights during Shabbat, as there is no vehicular traffic in the city anyway. About an hour and a quarter after Shabbat, the lights are turned on.

I am taking a Yiddish course in an adult education setting at the Zalman Shazar Center, named after the third president of Israel. The teacher, from Hebrew University, reminded the class, which numbers close to 100 people, of the classic book on the shtetl, *Life Is with People* by Mark Zborowski and Elizabeth Herzog, which I had read a long time ago. I decided that in Israel life is not only with people, but life is with food. I have never been to a meeting, social event, or gathering of any kind where food was not served – at least light refreshments. So, I shouldn't have been surprised that at a school program for mothers, held at an institute, a bag of food and drink was placed on each chair in the auditorium.

TUESDAY, MARCH 3, 2009

Today is the seventh of Adar, and my *ulpan* teacher announced that the rabbis and the Israeli government have designated this day as a *yahrtzeit* for Israel Defense Forces soldiers who have not yet been brought to burial – the Unknown Soldier. It also includes the men and women from Europe, the United States and many other countries who volunteered and fought for the State of Israel. Of course, the ancient significance of this date is the fact that it is Moshe Rabbeinu's birthday and *yahrtzeit*. His burial place is unknown, although he is thought to be interred near Mount Nevo where he died.

Several weeks ago, a bit after Tu B'Shvat, I had a chance to spend an hour walking in a beautiful Jewish National Fund forest near Hadassah Hospital. For years my basic Tu B'Shvat song, as taught to 100 preschoolers at the shul nursery and Sunday school, was "Hashkediya Porachat." This was the first time, however, that I actually saw a huge field of blooming almond trees with their pink blossoms and the beginnings of the almond fruit on their branches. Actually, the word *shaked* in Hebrew means "diligent," and these are the first trees to bloom around the Tu B'Shvat holiday when it's still winter here.

I recently learned that there is a men-only Chareidi unit in the army, which provides time for learning Torah, very strict food *hechsherim*, and includes a number of other amenities important to religious men. Apparently, many Modern Orthodox soldiers are also very comfortable in this unit and prefer to serve there. It was established for Chareidim who are basically exempt from serving in the military but who either wish to serve their country in a religious environment or would like to open up possibilities for future employment. Apparently, "Have you completed your military service?" is one of the first questions asked when applying to university or for various jobs.

The wedding season is now beginning as people who are engaged prefer not to wait for the seven weeks between Pesach and Shavuot when, with the exception of one or two days, people don't marry. My grandchildren, who are in *shidduchim*, are busy attending weddings, sometimes several per week. I was at the wedding of a Modern Orthodox couple, and there were about 800 guests, many of them in their 20s and 30s. Both *chatan* and *kallah* were from moshavim, so each invited the entire moshav. I was especially interested in the head coverings since they were different from those I'd seen at Chareidi weddings. About 90 percent of the men wore white knitted yarmulkes with a bit of colored decoration around the edge. The women wore turbans, snoods or pretty hats, which covered almost all of their hair.

Of course, everyone was modestly dressed. The Chareidi wedding attendees wear either turbans or sheitels, but with nary a hair showing. Of course, similarly modestly attired women generally have sleeves until just below the elbow, which is acceptable, although some prefer to keep their sleeves to their wrists. High necklines are de rigueur. My grandson explained to me that according to basic halachah, Sephardic and Modern Orthodox women are appropriately attired. Anyhow, I had an interesting lecture on how the law differs within various religious groups. And, by the way, I really enjoyed the kibbutz wedding, which held all the guests in a massive tent.

Friday, March 13, 2009

Purim was very festive. It's especially fun to see the children in their costumes and the adults relaxed and happy as they stroll in the streets. I celebrated two Purims – the first one in B'nei Brak with Shira and her family. Shira served the traditional meat *kreplach*. My mother used to say that you eat *kreplach* whenever you *shlug*. On Purim you beat Haman with the *groggers*; on Erev Yom Kippur you *shlug kaparos* by swinging the chicken, or money, three times around your head; and on Hoshana Rabbah you beat the myrtle branches on the ground.

Cities that were walled when the biblical leader Joshua conquered the Land of Israel celebrate Purim a day later, on Shushan Purim, the 15th of Adar. Jerusalem qualifies, and I hosted Shira's family at the *seudah* here. Her 19-year-old son, Menachem, invited a few yeshiva friends to sing and dance for some musical entertainment. Since many people travel from various sites in Israel to celebrate another Purim, in Jerusalem, the Egged buses were out in full force to ferry the crowds to our holy city. Where there is doubt as to whether a city was considered walled in the time of Joshua, two days of Purim are kept. Two examples are Teverya and Chevron. Taanit Esther is observed by all on the 13th of Adar.

Purim is the major gift-giving holiday here, not Chanukah. So, *mishloach manot*, large trays of delectable edibles, and often wine, sometimes with a pretty dish or other item, are exchanged. This year I gave close to 20 people, and that took some planning. Fortunately, Shira came with her son Shmuel, and they delivered many of the baskets for me. The mitzvah is to give at least two foods that require different brachot. I should add that Purim is a big day for giving *tzedakah*, and my doorbell was constantly ringing, allowing me to fulfill this mitzvah.

When returning from B'nei Brak to Jerusalem on Purim, I had the chance to try a *kasher le-mehadrin* bus. I don't know how many people are aware that there are buses with separate seating in Monsey, New York, and also some buses that transport people to New York City. Not to be outdone, Jerusalem and B'nei Brak have their share of these buses as well.

One pleasure I enjoy here is the availability of *rimonim* (pomegranates) for many months, well past Rosh HaShanah when they are first enjoyed. By the way, *rimon* is also the word for "hand grenade" in Modern Hebrew, perhaps because it is shaped very much like the fruit. Or maybe it comes from the modern French *grenade*, which means "pomegranate." Another insight occurs to me. Most of my life I have been somewhat annoyed by rain, especially when it interfered with some plans. However, I find myself rejoicing when the rain falls, as it is a blessing we pray for daily at this time of year. Especially now, every drop is necessary. So, I've become a bit more Israeli.

Monday, March 30, 2009

As a guest at many Shabbat *seudot*, I have learned that there is a pecking order when the head of the table distributes the *Kiddush* wine and then the challah. It seems that after he takes a sip of the wine or a bite of the challah, his wife, who may be seated at the other end of the table, is the first to be served; then, an important older person, maybe a mother-in-law or grandmother; then a distinguished guest; and then the children, in order of descending age until the youngest child tastes the wine and then the challah. I'm comfortable with this ritual.

It is especially delightful to see how my Sephardic neighbors, who have a table full of children and grandchildren, observe this practice; I am generally served right after the mother! At the end of Shabbat I am also treated to a Sephardic *Havdalah*, which contains the basic *brachot* – like the Ashkenazic one with which I am familiar – but which takes much longer.

Today, I had lunch with a friend whose daughter and family are Belzer Chassidim. I imagine you realize that there are differences in *minhagim* between Chassidim and Mitnagdim. There are, of course, variations within these subgroups as well. My friend described the courtship details of her grandchildren. First, both sets of parents check out the intended match. Second, both sets of parents meet each other. Third, the girl's parents meet the boy, and vice versa. Finally, the girl and boy meet once for a half hour, after not even having talked on the phone. If they agree, the match is finalized. Since the couple expects to be supported during at least the first year, there is a financial commitment and it's heavily weighted on the girl's side. For example, her family agrees to pay for the wedding and, usually, half the rent for the first year of marriage, plus they often buy the furniture and appliances. Then, the big expense is purchasing the apartment, which sometimes falls completely on the girl's parents and sometimes is shared by both sides.

Of course the various ceremonies include a *l'chayim* – a small festive gathering for close family and a few friends – which usually takes place the same night that the couple has met and agreed, and it doesn't last longer than an hour or so. Several days later there is the *vort*, usually a large event to celebrate the engagement. It is called a *vort*—which in Yiddish means "word"—because it is then that the young man and woman give their word and formally commit to marry, and because the chatan traditionally shares words of Torah with the well-wishers. For the Belzer, as with all Orthodox wedding preparations, the young *chatan* and *kallah* each spends time between the engagement and the wedding studying the laws of marital purity, the general obligations of the mates, and the importance of *shalom bayit* (domestic harmony). These studies are conducted privately with a marriage coach.

Following the wedding, there are six more nights of *Sheva Brachot* where both sides of the family entertain a number of people, including if possible at least a minyan of men, and it's customary to include *panim chadashot*, someone who has not attended the wedding.

My friend says her married grandchildren, who were wed in the

Chassidic fashion, are very happy and in the last two weeks she gained three great-grandchildren, making a total of seven since the spate of weddings over the last three years.

Sunday, April 19, 2009

This year I spent Pesach in London with my two sons, celebrating the first seder with Hillel and the second with Rashi. Although I actually celebrate only one seder because I live in Israel, I did enjoy being with the family at their second one.

There were a few interesting differences from my past seder experiences, notably, at Hillel's home I participated in my first Lubavitch seder. Some distinctions included:

- The sons, in addition to the father, had their own seder plates;
- On the seder plate were chicory (maror), kohlrabi (karpas), shank bone (zeroa), roasted egg (beitzah) and onion (chazeret);
- The matzah was not eaten at the table. All attendees needed to move back about a foot so that no possible crumbs would fall on the tablecloth, and we were actually given a plastic bag to catch any crumbs that did escape while eating;
- The Haggadah omits the last three or four songs, such as "Chad Gadya", "Echad Mi Yodea" and "Adir Hu";
- Every fruit or vegetable used is peeled, even the mushrooms;
- The Mah Nishtanah (The Four Questions) were recited in Yiddish and Hebrew by all present, including the head of the seder asking himself all the questions.

Those were some of the new experiences for me. There was plenty of singing and discussion by everyone. To me, it was an amazing feat for the food to be prepared from scratch, including horseradish, mayonnaise, and even home-roasted coffee beans. The family even juices their own fruit—only peelable ones, of course—and the members of this household don't eat any matzah meal products.

An interesting friend of Rashi's is Rabbi Kestenbaum from London, who makes the only oat matzah in the world. As I have two family members who are allergic to wheat products, they of course ate only oat matzah, which is quite expensive. It is distributed in many countries, including Israel, the United States (where it is listed in the *OU Guide to Passover*), South Africa,

Australia, Belgium and Canada.

I also experienced some unusual (for me) davening on several occasions at the Adeni shul. This congregation stems from Aden, Yemen, and Hillel tells me they are a mixture of Yemenite and Sephardic. There are three such shuls in London and a number in Israel. I could hardly follow the service, which included the entire *Shir HaShirim* and numerous chants – often, but not always, in unison. Their pronunciation of Hebrew is very different, so I considered these services a cultural immersion.

Last but not least, I learned of a new end-of-Pesach ritual. On the Shabbat following Pesach my daughter-in-law Ruthie, who is an outstanding challah baker, made her challah in the shape of a large key. Now, I have made numerous round challot for Rosh HaShana, and challah in the shape of the Ten Commandments for Shavuot, but this was an unfamiliar shape. My son explained that the key symbolizes *Hashem* opening the gates of *parnassa* for people, since produce is planted early and the hope is that the harvest after Pesach will yield its abundance. Some bake the *shlissel challah* with an actual key inside, others make it in the shape of a key, and there are those who put sesame seeds on top in the form of a key.

By the way, we are now counting the Omer so my usually clean-shaven menfolk are growing beards. That, along with no major music festivities, constitutes some of the customs for Ashkenazim, at least until Lag BaOmer or the first of the Hebrew month of Sivan. Some hold this period of semi-mourning until three days before Shavuot.

Sunday, May 31, 2009

My *ulpan* teacher says the weather between Pesach and Shavuot is always variable. Indeed, it is either hotter or cooler than is usual for the season. After Shavuot, however, when listening to the weather forecast one will almost always hear the word *chom*, meaning "heat" (also "fever"). I should reiterate that the heat here is very dry and evenings are usually cool and pleasant.

On Shavuot I learned that the Jerusalem Talmud lists only the wheat harvest as *bikurim* (first fruits) since it is the only harvest that is completed by Shavuot. Produce was brought to the Holy Temple between Sukkot and Chanukah. I also discovered that in addition to the familiar names of this festival—Chag HaKatzir (the Festival of Harvest), Zman Matan Torateinu (the time of the giving of our Torah), Chag HaBikurim (the Festival of the First Fruits, meaning the wheat) and Chag HaShavuot (the Festival of Weeks)—Israelis use the biblical words *Regel*, since it is one of the Shalosh Regalim (three pilgrimage holidays), and *Atzeret* (from the root word "stop"), since it ends the period of the Omer that began with Pesach.

At the entrance to the Old City in East Jerusalem, there is now a beautiful, elegant mall called Mamilla. My granddaughter Elisheva, who is now completing her second year in Jerusalem—this one as a dorm counselor in a seminary for American girls — joined me at a restaurant on the newly constructed second floor. We were afforded a picturesque view of a large area of the Old City.

I recently needed to go to a framer near the Hadassah College in downtown Jerusalem. Since I had to wait until my picture was ready, I had some time to explore the Russian Compound, its large church (I only saw the outside) and the city prison. My return home was greatly delayed by the Pope's visit. Streets were blocked and traffic rerouted. In addition, a well-known rabbi was interred, and the funeral procession was lengthy. The *minhag* in Jerusalem is that the dead are buried immediately. No waiting, not even for relatives to fly in.

The daughter of my Shabbat hosts told me that she lives and teaches in Yerucham, a small town in the Negev about 70 miles south of Jerusalem. To get from there to any other part of the country, one needs to travel to Beer Sheva and then catch a bus to the desired destination. However, there is a religious man who operates a small van that will bring passengers directly from Yerucham to Jerusalem. He studies there for about five hours and then, in the late afternoon, returns people to Yerucham. I think he is quite enterprising.

Tuesday, June 28, 2009

The post offices in Jerusalem (maybe even in all of Israel) will not hold your mail. Since I travel often, I'm fortunate to have helpful neighbors.

After a very wonderful journey to the States, I found five wedding invitations in my mail. As I have noted previously, the period between Shavuot and the 17th of Tammuz – which initiates The Three Weeks – is the shortest interval in the year when it is appropriate to celebrate weddings. One invitation was to the wedding of the granddaughter of Rabbi Simcha

Kook and great-granddaughter of Israel's first chief rabbi, Abraham Isaac Kook. Rabbi Simcha Kook, Chief Rabbi of Rechovot, was recently chosen to head the newly renovated Churvah Synagogue in Jerusalem's Old City.

At the Jerusalem Theater last week I enjoyed a marvelous *chazanut* concert combining four young *chazanim*, a small musical ensemble and a men's choir. Two of my favorites – *non-chazanut* pieces – are "Mameh" and Rossini's "Figaro" theme song medley, both in Yiddish. However, instead of saying Figaro, the singer called him "shvigaro," a pun on the Yiddish word *shviger* (mother-in-law).

Chassidim, one of the various groups within the Chareidi world, have many sub-groups. In the United States, most people recognize the Lubavitcher (Chabad) Chassidim. Here in Israel, the most well-known groups are Belz, Vizhnitz, Gur, Bobov, Modzitz, and Breslov. However, there are many Chassidic rebbes originating from lesser-known small towns in Poland, with fewer devotees, such as the Radziner Rebbe, The Munkatcher Rebbe, the Rachmastrivka Rebbe, and the Nadvorna Rebbe, to name but a few. In Bayit VeGan we have the Amshinover Rebbe, who is well known for his popular "minyan factory," and the Sochatchover Rebbe, who presides in my next-door shul.

I was thinking of the number of children in Chareidi families. In a very subjective, unscientific study of the number of families I know personally – about 30 – the average per household is eight or nine children. Subsequently, I read in a newspaper that my personal evaluation was statistically accurate.

Throughout Israel, there are many apartments that are in the process of being built for young couples. When I first arrived here I thought it was unusual that when purchasing a home, say for $100,000, the buyer needs at least $80,000 in cash up front and may take only a small mortgage from the bank. This is in contrast to America where a much smaller down payment is needed. Hence, Israel suffers less from the housing crisis.

"Only in Israel" is a label I amusingly attach to certain facts and incidents that I discover or hear about. For example, recently on a Friday night I met a pretty, alert, elderly woman who has 54 great-grandchildren. I was impressed. In addition, that evening I learned a few anecdotes:

A plumber came to repair an item and noticed the husband and son studying *Mishnayot*, so he sat down and joined them in learning.

Shortly before Pesach, a bus driver stopped his bus near the large Jerusalem Machaneh Yehudah market where some rabbis were busily writing contracts. He jumped off the bus and returned three minutes later, telling the passengers, "I just sold my *chametz*."

Some passengers in a taxi stopped to buy *schach* for their sukkah. They were concerned as to whether it would fulfill the halachic requirements. The taxi driver joined the conversation and opined that he thought the *schach* was not kosher.

Finally, a friend said that her taxi driver wasn't wearing a *kippa*, but when he needed to drink some water from the ever-present bottle carried by almost everyone here, he put on his *kippa*, said a *bracha*, and then removed it after drinking. The line between religious and unobservant people is not always clearly drawn.

Friday, July 17, 2009

I recently returned from a very *nachesdig* bar mitzvah of my grandson Yehuda Aharon in London. I was so pleased that besides being a family reunion, for the first time since Ed's first *yahrtzeit*, some friends from Lafayette were able to attend. A day or two later, another Lafayette friend joined us for Yehuda's *siyum* on the Talmudic Tractate *Makot*, which he had learned all year. It was supportive for me to have my friends join in the *simcha*.

An ad in the newspaper caught my eye, as it featured an appealing meat sandwich at a newly opened deli. The caption read: "Last Chance before the Nine Days." The kosher meat restaurants do little business during the nine days before Tisha B'Av. Sephardim hold that only during the week in which Tisha B'Av falls do they refrain from eating meat. However, Ashkenazim refrain from eating meat all nine days, except for Shabbat.

Wednesday, August 12, 2009

My neighborhood was founded about 70 years ago and designated as an educational area. The streets abound with schools, mostly religious, including the well-known high school, Boys Town Jerusalem, and the Kol Torah Yeshiva, both of which have their own campuses and dormitories. So the sounds of children going to and from school permeate the area. When I first lived here in 1972-73, the neighborhood was about 10 percent Chareidi, 50 percent Modern Orthodox and 40 percent secular. Over the years, it has become "chareidified" and is now about 70 percent Chareidi, 20 percent Modern Orthodox and 10 percent secular. As mentioned, there are many shuls, and when passing by one can listen to the various melodies and styles of davening. I live on one of the three main thoroughfares in Bayit VeGan; in addition to several bus lines, this street has the most pedestrian traffic, since it is full of shops, schools, banks and offices and, therefore, normal everyday sounds.

Living by the rhythms of Jewish time is still full of surprises. Erev Shabbat, several hours before candle lighting, the stores close and there is almost complete silence as people are indoors preparing. Of course, on Shabbat itself when the area is closed to vehicular traffic, we hear the sounds of people walking and talking and children playing.

I recently noticed another period of silence: during the minutes right after the Tisha B'Av fast ends, when people are indoors breaking their fasts, the neighborhood is eerily quiet. I should also add that some shops are closed all day on Tisha B'Av, and some just in the morning so people can daven.

After Tisha B'Av, Shira and her family vacationed at my home. A well-kept secret from many is the location of the charming and verdant Jerusalem Botanical Gardens, situated in the quiet, unassuming neighborhood of Nayot. My B'nei Brak family and I spent a riveting two hours there today. There is a train ride, which includes a tour leader explaining the various trees, vegetation and many other items imported from around the globe. Following this tour, we visited the butterfly house and heard an enlightening lecture about butterflies, their habits and habitats. The vegetation was well signed and we walked around enjoying the atmosphere very much. This was an area so convenient for us to access, and the pleasant experience was well worth the time invested.

I recently visited Sussya, a small village about 40 miles southwest of Jerusalem. It contains an amazingly well-preserved, large mosaic synagogue floor that is at least 1,300 years old. In addition, the area features remains of homes and mikvaot of its ancient inhabitants. I also visited Kibbutz Kfar Etzion, which has a more stirring modern history. It is an example of the very recent privatization that many kibbutzim are currently undergoing. As part of my day, I picnicked in Yatir, the largest forest in Israel, which had a sizable reservoir, very depleted in these dry summer months, but impressive nevertheless. The last stop on my tour was a visit to a small winery. Israel is famous for its wineries, with each section of the country growing its own types of grapes. There are more than 250 wineries manufacturing over 33 million bottles annually. Of these, 150 are boutique wineries that produce less than 100,000 bottles per year. The winery I visited is family founded and owned. They produce a mere 4,000 bottles a year. This tour was also taken with Shira and family.

Another visit I recently enjoyed was as a guest of Ruti and Avi Golan in Midreshet Sde Boker, which is the agricultural laboratory affiliated with Ben-Gurion University in Beer Sheva. During my visit, I had a chance to participate in an international piano workshop. It was exciting to listen to the talented performers and then hear them being critiqued by master teachers.

The Golans have a very pretty home. One interesting feature is that the kitchen counters and floors are cut from the ancient stones of the nearby massive crater, which was formed millions of years ago by erosion. Embedded in the polished stones are fossils that are 123 million years old. Wow!

Avi, a plant biochemist, commutes to Beer Sheva to teach. He told me something of his own research. He has a small but rare grove of pistachio trees containing seven different species. It is the largest such collection in the world. He needs the seeds for three more species to complete his collection of the genus Pistacia. These seeds can only be obtained from Turkey and Iran, and he is having trouble acquiring them due to international bureaucratic procedures. In the 1980s Israel exported missiles to Iran and imported pistachios in return. Obviously, that is not possible today. Incidentally, next to oil, pistachios are Iran's major export, and they are its largest producers in the world followed by California, Turkey and Syria.

Pistachios, although one of Israelis' favorite nuts, are not grown locally, perhaps because the trees take thirteen years to blossom and Israelis don't have the patience to wait! We now buy them from Turkey. Pistachios are healthy since they contain magnesium, iron and protein. In Modern Hebrew, pistachio is *fistuk*, which is etymologically very similar to the English word. Avi cited an interesting biblical reference [Genesis 43:11], which was confirmed by my sons, Rabbis Rashi and Hillel. Yaakov (our forefather Jacob) sent a gift of *botnim* to Tzafnat Paneach (his son Yosef's Egyptian name), the vizier of Egypt. Although in Modern Hebrew *botnim* are peanuts, in biblical Hebrew they are pistachios, as is evidenced by the biblical commentator Rashi who writes the word in Old French. Peanuts are from the New World; hence they were unknown in ancient times. Since pistachios aren't native to Israel, Avi suggests that Yaakov acquired them from Mesopotamia and thought that they would be an appropriate gift for Pharaoh's second in command.

Sunday, August 30, 2009

Last week, my grandson Simcha (son of Rashi and Ruthie in London) and I enjoyed a vocal concert by the famous singer Avraham Fried. He performed right outside the Old City Walls, in a deep canyon formerly named Gei-Hinnom, which is Gehenom in Yiddish and Hell in English. In ancient times, this valley was the site where pagans slaughtered their children as sacrifices to their idols. Later, the name was changed to Breichat HaSultan, the Sultan's Pool. Now, when there is no water in evidence, there is an amazing amphitheater containing about 5,000 seats. Part of the area still has the ancient massive stone seats (steps). Avraham Fried was accompanied by a small male choir and a musical combo, complete with colorful spotlights. Two themes ran through some of his songs: the holiness of Jerusalem and the weightiness of the month of Elul (as we prepare to be judged on Rosh HaShanah). I still find it startling to see groups of men, who are total strangers and know the *Maariv* service by heart, band together to spontaneously form a minyan right in the amphitheater.

Simcha and I also enjoyed a concert by world-famous clarinet player Giora Feidman. His group's show was held in a fascinating venue called The Valley of the Communities, a stone amphitheater in Yad Vashem. The names of hundreds of communities decimated in the Holocaust were engraved on the various walls. It was a sobering experience to walk through the several stone chambers. The concert, however, which touched on the Holocaust, was in the main very *freilach*.

My other recent musical event was a show featuring Dudu Fisher singing so many beloved and new Yiddish songs. Some were liturgical ("Avinu Malkeinu"), some were from the Second Avenue National Yiddish Theater in New York ("Bai Mir Bist Du Shein"), and some were klezmer tunes by his support klezmer band. The Jerusalem Theater was full.

If you can deal with a true Israeli experience: the proletariat crowds; the sound of vendors hawking their wares; the smell of fresh produce; newly baked challot; live fish; pungent spices—all brightly colored; and most of all if you like bargains, THEN, the place to be in Jerusalem is the venerable marketplace, Machaneh Yehudah, on Friday afternoon. That is when you will receive efficient service, a warm "Shabbat Shalom" and best of all, lowest prices, as all the vendors (by the way, I only saw male sellers) want to reduce their stock before Shabbat.

Tuesday, September 29, 2009

The annulment of vows, before Rosh HaShanah, was a new custom for me. At one of my *shiurim*, three invited religious men formed a *beit din* (a Jewish rabbinical court). A group of about 150 women of all ages, students in the class, stood up and read, in English, a few paragraphs spelling out the various types of promises or vows they had made that they regretted. The men then answered with a ritual Hebrew paragraph, nullifying these vows. My grandsons Menachem and Saadia told me that shortly before Rosh HaShanah a group of four boys, in their respective yeshivot, gather together. Three act as a *beit din* and listen to the fourth; then they rotate, giving each one an opportunity to have his vows annulled. This ceremony is called *hatarat nedarim*.

During Yom Kippur I experienced the quietest day of the year. Everybody was in shul or resting. There was hardly a soul outside and of course no traffic, as on Shabbat. And absolutely nothing was going on in the evening, as people were breaking their fasts and recovering from the day. I learned that on Yom Kippur it is more important to fast than to go to shul, even if you have to stay in bed all day. Of course, those who need to eat for health reasons are permitted to do so. There is a well-documented maximum amount of food or drink allowed for various medical conditions.

Following my grandson Yehuda's bar mitzvah in London in July, my family celebrated the bar mitzvah of my youngest Israeli grandson, Shmuel, in B'nei Brak. I am always a little startled by the davening times. They start at 7:30 a.m. and finish about 10:20. We really had to get there early to participate in the full service. I remember when we first came to Lafayette in 1960, the shul services started at 7:30 a.m., since most of the attendees were businessmen who needed to open their stores by 9:00.

At the celebratory party several days later, in addition to the continuous smile on my grandson's face, Rashi and Hillel gave very impressive speeches in fluent Hebrew, and Ronit's husband, Boruch, also gave a fine *drasha* in English. We were very proud of Shmuel's excellent rendition of the *haftarah* and the achievements of the entire family. Adding to the festivities, several former Hoosiers joined in the *simcha*, making it a mini Lafayette reunion.

My hostess at a recent Shabbat meal is about 38 years old. She has 10 children ranging in age from 2 to 16 and has had five miscarriages. She told me that she had to call five hospitals in Jerusalem and Tel Aviv to find a physician who would take care of her most recent miscarriage without removing her uterus. Apparently, non-religious women are usually comfortable with the idea of a hysterectomy following an abortion or miscarriage. However, my friend, like many religious women, wants the option of having more children. She told me of an organization that collects money to provide women who plan to have abortions with the financial means to purchase all the necessary supplies and equipment to care for the impending baby. Apparently, many thousands of abortions are carried out in Israel each year, and this institute, called Puah (after the midwife in Egypt who saved the Jewish babies from their fate in the Nile), claims credit for averting a significant number of them. Quite interesting! Also worth mentioning is that Israel has very advanced fertility clinics to help women conceive.

I was recently at a Sephardic *brit* of my upstairs neighbors' grandson. They have 14 children, *bli ayin hara*, and one of their younger daughters gave birth to a baby boy. Of course the event was held in a large hall, and I was so impressed that, as far as I could count, all 14 children with their spouses and families were in attendance. One of the advantages of living here is the ability to attend many family functions without traveling long distances. I noticed that the men kissed one another on both cheeks. Cheek kissing is a common greeting in many cultures, though I've rarely seen it in the United States.

Another interesting fact is that most people tend to make a *brit* early in the morning. My son Rabbi Rashi told me that this is learned from Avraham Avinu who arose early to take his son, Yitzchak (Isaac), to be sacrificed. The commentator Rashi makes a two-word comment (in Hebrew) on the wording of the *pasuk*, "And Avraham got up early in the morning." He says, "He hurried to do the mitzvah." This is why people perform a *brit* as early in the day as is feasible. Ed used to say, "One should run to do mitzvot."

Some people make a *brit* in the afternoon, if it is more convenient for guests to come. Morning or afternoon, a full meat meal is generally served.

Thursday, October 8, 2009

My Israeli grandsons Menachem and Mordechai, and my London granddaughter Brocha, who is studying here this year in seminary, built me a lovely sukkah on my porch. I especially remember my husband Ed at this time, since he devoted so much time, thought and planning for our large Lafayette sukkah. I recall the many friends who stopped in to visit all through the years. Ed died on *Chol HaMo'ed* Sukkot, so we'll be going to the cemetery right after the *chag*. There's a custom not to visit the cemetery on *Yom Tov*, even on *chol hamo'ed*. All my children and some grandchildren will be joining me.

People who stem from Poland continue to observe a little known Sukkot ritual. As you know, we welcome seven *ushpizin*, a different one each night, into our sukkot. If a person's name happens to be the same as one of these *ushpizin*, then that individual would serve a lovely meal to another nine invited men, on the specific night that has his namesake. So, if your name is Avraham, Yitzchak, Yaakov, Yosef, Moshe, Aharon, or David, the night that "guest" is welcomed would be your night to entertain in your sukkah.

It is customary for men to sleep, as well as eat, in the sukkah. So here, as in many religious neighborhoods, sukkot are quite large. Some families even have two: one for sleeping and one for eating. The weather here has been very comfortable over the *chag*, and I haven't seen a single bee.

Thursday, October 22, 2009

Some years ago, a Galitzianer-Litvak marriage was considered mixed. In Israel, a Sephardi-Ashkenazi union is still considered mixed. My family is now in the process of adjusting to just such a blended union, as my grandson Menachem, who recently turned 20, will soon be marrying a girl of Iraqi-Moroccan descent. The rituals of both groups are very different, but the custom is that the bride adopts her husband's traditions, and that is what will be happening in this situation. They had a lively *eirusin* (engagement party) including some intriguing Oriental songs and melodies, as well as a henna ceremony, in which the bride's hands and face are adorned with a colorful, removable dye made from crushed henna leaves. This is done to ward off the evil eye. Merav, the *kallah*, was decked out in a royal robe and looked very pretty. All the jewelry, I was told, must be gold. The ceremony took place last week, with the wedding scheduled for early December. I imagine the amalgam of customs will be interesting.

Just last night, my granddaughter Yocheved, Rashi and Ruthie's daughter, called from London, asked me if I'd like a new grandson and very joyfully announced her engagement. The wedding is tentatively planned for March. Her *chatan*, Yehoshua Wechsler, is English, from a fine London family, and has been learning in yeshiva in Israel for the last three years. Yocheved has been teaching Bible, Hebrew and Jewish History in a London high school. More details to follow.

THURSDAY, NOVEMBER 5, 2009

Two weeks ago, on the evening that Yocheved and Yehoshua's engagement was confirmed, there was a *l'chayim* in England, a quick gathering of about 50 people. Several days later the *vort* was held, a massive festive gathering of over 400 guests celebrating the engagement, and there were many appropriate speeches.

Sometimes the *tenaim* document is signed at a *vort*. This is a mutual agreement between the two sets of parents for the date and financial conditions of the forthcoming marriage of their children. In most religious circles, volumes of the Talmud are given to the bridegroom, and the bride-to-be is gifted with jewelry.

I was privileged to host a *l'chayim* here in Jerusalem when Yocheved visited for a few days last week. This was an opportunity to become acquainted with Yehoshua's grandparents, aunts, uncles and other family members who live in Jerusalem. Many of Yocheved's friends from her seminary days, all married and sporting lovely sheitels, as well as other guests attended. Yehoshua and his *rav* (teacher) gave inspiring *divrei Torah*.

The Shabbat before a wedding, Ashkenazim usually sponsor a *Kiddush* in honor of the *aufruf*, when the *chatan* is called up to the Torah and showered with sweets.

On the topic of celebrations, one evening last week my upstairs neighbors called and invited me to a *hillulah*. As I was unfamiliar with the term, my neighbor said to come to her apartment in two hours to commemorate the *yahrtzeit* of Rachel Imeinu, our foremother Rachel. Well, about 6 of the 14 children with their spouses, and assorted guests were assembled for a full course, delicious meal. The host gave a meaningful and inspiring lecture about Rachel, and there was some singing. And so I celebrated my first *hillulah*.

Thursday, November 12, 2009

Thanksgivig is approaching and some American expatriates still celebrate the holiday here. The Hebrew term is Chag HaHodaya – literally, "the holiday of thanks." The context in which I initially learned this term was at a *seudat hodaya*, a thanksgiving meal, prepared by a person who miraculously survived a near catastrophe and to which friends and family were invited.

Over 30 years ago, some friends volunteered for a time on Kibbutz Sde Eliyahu. Recently, they were given a private tour of the now thriving kibbutz, which is economically sound because of a successful beehive business. Also, some of the members have found a way to save the 40 percent of their alfalfa crop, which was formerly eaten by rodents. They have built special birdhouses for the white barn owl and the kestrel whose natural diet is rodents. However, since the kibbutz is near the Jordanian border, and the birds knew no boundaries, they would fly back and forth from Jordan. Some Jordanians, upon seeing the white owls flapping their wings, thought they were a harbinger of death and would shoot them. So, the farmers from the kibbutz went to Jordan and explained to them how their own alfalfa crops would be much more plentiful if they would welcome the birds. The Israelis showed the Jordanians how to build proper birdhouses, and the economies of both areas have improved. It is peaceful international cooperation at its best!

You probably know that many or most Israeli kibbutzim have been privatized. However, Sde Eliyahu in the Beit She'an Valley, and Lavi in the north—both Orthodox kibbutzim— retain their traditional kibbutz status.

Motzaei Shabbat, December 5, 2009

This has been an especially *freilach* week with the wedding of my grandson Menachem and his bride, Merav. It was a joyous event. What was unusual was the mix of Ashkenazic and Sephardic wedding tunes and ritual wedding dances. The hundreds of guests of different backgrounds were compatible, and the energetic dancing and creative shtick of the young people was fun to watch. The wedding celebrations continued through the week with nightly *Sheva Brachot*. I hosted 25 people for three Shabbat meals. The singing and *divrei Torah* added to the festive occasion. It was startling for me to hear the very different chants that the Sephardic guests used.

Shira's daughter Tovah and Hillels's daughter Brocha prepared and served the exceptionally delicious Shabbat food. Ed used to say, "Never go anywhere without a *d'var Torah* in your back pocket," and I am proud to say that a number of my grandchildren offered original and impressive speeches. Generally speaking, Sephardim are especially thrilled when a son is born. Hence, when saying *l'hitraot* (hope we meet again soon) to my new granddaughter's aunt, upon her family's departing from my Shabbat *Sheva Brachot*, her response was, "We'll meet next at the *brit*."

The week continued with various families hosting other *Sheva Brachot*. It is necessary to have a minyan, so each event featured at least 20 people. At each party, it's customary to invite *panim chadashot*. The Sephardic custom is to invite two new people, while Ashkenazim invite one.

I have noticed a number of young girls, in B'nei Brak and other areas, sporting long, heavy, single braids of hair down their backs. My daughter Shira pointed out that since these girls will likely cut their hair when they marry and wear sheitels, they keep their hair long in their youth. It is more modest to braid the hair than to let it lie loose. Another reason for the braid, particularly on Shabbat, is that since brushing hair is not permissible on Shabbat, as some hairs are pulled out from their roots, a braid can be tidier and will not unravel the next day.

As I have mentioned previously, the term Chareidim encompasses a vast number of different groups, many with their distinctive customs. I recently learned a unique trait of Gerer Chassidim: they never cut their *payot*. Some just let them hang down, while others raise them from the temples and tie them under their especially large yarmulkes, making them not visible from the outside. By the way, although there is a plethora of Chassidic groups in Israel, the Gerer Chassidim (as they are referred to in Yiddish) are the largest. They can also be called Chassidei Gur (the term in Hebrew), named for the town near Warsaw where they originate.

Thursday, December 14, 2009

Last week, I went to the center of Jerusalem with my house guest, a friend from West Lafayette. As we were approaching the theater to enjoy a concert of Baroque music, *The Songs of Solomon and David*, we had to walk a short unexpected distance to our destination since many of the streets were cordoned off for a demonstration against Prime Minister Netanyahu for enforcing the freeze on housing construction. We heard there were an estimated 10,000 demonstrators. Our taxi driver pointed out five identical vehicles in a row, one of which the Prime Minister was riding in. This was a protective device against would-be terrorists since they wouldn't be able to identify Netanyahu's vehicle. Of course, these large vans had flashing lights and were given the right of way by all the stopped traffic. Our driver added that President Peres had two identical vehicles for the same purpose. The concert consisted of lovely music by a Baroque ensemble playing medieval melodies to Psalms, Chronicles and Song of Songs. My guest and I enjoyed the evening.

Chanukah is a time of good cheer and good will. Some friends were running to get on a bus and they reached the stop just as the bus was pulling out. However, it halted a few meters ahead and the door opened. The driver said, "I did this favor for you because it's Chanukah."

I was riding with a Chareidi taxi driver to Lod, a city located about 45 minutes from Jerusalem. The man asked why I was traveling to Lod, and I replied, "For a Chanukah party at my recently married grandson's new apartment." He asked, "Will there be a minyan there?" I asked him to wait, and upon our arrival I checked with my grandson. Menachem said he would try to get a few neighbors, and we took the cab driver's phone number. After about 20 minutes, Menachem called him and said, "Come, you'll be the 10th man." So, not only did the driver not have to daven *Mincha* alone but he also helped make up the Chanukah party minyan.

Wednesday, December 23, 2009

I spent a lovely day in Tel Aviv, visiting the beautiful art museum, which is part of a complex of amazing, architecturally interesting structures, such as the Azrieli Towers and the Tel Aviv Opera House. Particularly impressive was a pottery exhibit, which featured a variety of creative pieces crafted by Israeli artists. I also noted the vast selection of kosher restaurants located in the immediate area.

I completed this really nice day out with participating in my Jerusalem weekly Yiddish club, which includes about 30 people. The recent program featured a klezmer trio, and of course I *kvelled* recognizing every one of their *nigunim* from my Lafayette Klezmorim repertoire. Interestingly, the leader and clarinet player is a direct descendant of the Rebbe Elimelech—for those who are familiar with that popular song—and the accordionist comes from Belz, which is one of the klezmer Yiddish favorites, "Mayn Shtetl Belz."

I've been learning about differences within Israeli society, primarily in the Orthodox spectrum. I think I'm just scratching the surface, but the variety of customs is interesting. For example: Those who wear knitted yarmulkes (Modern Orthodox) disagree with the Chareidim in a number of ways. They are happy with Ashkenazi-Sephardi matches, they serve in the army, they adhere to different *hechsherim* for their kosher food, they dress differently, and they are very Zionistic and prioritize the State of Israel. The Chareidim have differences among the various groups of Chassidim and Mitnagdim. In fact, they couldn't work together on many issues, so they are represented by two distinct Chareidi parties in the Knesset. To some of them, Zionism is not their favorite word. There is also a subgroup called Chareidi Leumi, known by the acronym Chardal. This describes a community that follows most Chareidi customs but will support the government by celebrating Yom HaAtzmaut and will go to live in towns across the Green Line. The women dress a bit more flamboyantly than standard Chareidi women. They may wear skirts to their ankles or don brightly colored snoods or turbans. They tend to be wholesome, very sincere, and display a flexible, independent approach. The men make up a large contingent of the Nachal Chareidi, a growing Chareidi unit in the army established in 1999. This serves to deflect some criticism from other segments of the population.

I learned another fact I had never noticed. To me, a black hat was just that. My friend suggested that if I ever see various groups of religious Jews together and I look closely, I'll see some hats are high, some brims wider, some hats more round, and others set slightly differently. Each hat is worn by a particular Orthodox group. The various garbs of different Chassidic groups are obvious, and I can even identify some by their appearance.

Interestingly, continuing my previous sensitivity to tensions within various groups, I noticed that in Kiryat Yovel, a mostly secular Jerusalem suburb adjacent to Bayit VeGan, when more Chareidi families attempted to settle there, both the Modern Orthodox and the secular groups did not welcome these newcomers. However, when a new *mikveh* was planned for the area, the Modern Orthodox and secular communities parted company. The *mikveh*, after all, is a given all across the Orthodox spectrum.

Chapter 3

2010

Thursday, January 7, 2010

Recently, when I attended an Emunah meeting, a woman whom I slightly recognized said, "Do you realize that we are somewhat related?" As you can imagine, I was really startled. Well, the connection is from my soon-to-be grandson, Yocheved's fiancé, Yehoshua Wechsler. This lady is his great-aunt.

Emunah is a Jewish women's organization similar to Amit, Hadassah, and others, and it supports many worthy projects in Israel. I belong to the English-speaking chapter, and in fact, many of the ladies hail from Great Britain.

A friend from Chicago, who stayed with me for several days recently, was kind enough to accompany me to visit Ed's grave, on a hilltop overlooking a panoramic view of Jerusalem. Sadly, a Holocaust survivor was recently interred nearby and my friend pointed out a custom common to many Holocaust survivors buried here. At the foot of his tombstone were the names of his immediate family who were killed by the Nazis and thus have no graves. Since the Torah declares, "You are dust, and to dust you shall return," these relatives are symbolically interred in the Holy Land.

Wednesday, January 20, 2010

I have recently returned from spending several days in London, where my son

Hillel, his wife Yael, and their family celebrated two *smachot*. My grandson Mendy became a bar mitzvah; two days earlier his mother gave birth to a lovely baby girl named Elisheva Liba Rivka. Mendy *leined*, flawlessly, the entire *Parshat Va-eira* from the Torah scroll that my family and friends donated to Rashi's shul in the name of my late husband, Ed (Yitzchak Isaac). The Torah was brought to the home of Hillel's next-door neighbor where the Shabbat service took place. Yael had given birth at home, with a midwife in attendance, so she was easily able to take part in the Shabbat bar mitzvah ceremonies. All the festivities proceeded beautifully, including the *Melaveh Malkah* in the hall of London's Great Synagogue.

Monday, February 15, 2010

Today, mid-February, we have a *chamsin* (Arabic) or *sharav* (Hebrew). The 75 degree temperature will probably continue for several more days. I was told this weather front is a hot, dry wind from the East. I understand there was real wintry weather in many parts of the States.

Last week, I had a wonderful view from my window of a *Hachnasat Sefer Torah*. A family from Sao Paulo, Brazil, donated a *Sefer Torah* to the yeshiva across the street from my house. I have participated in several such events, but what distinguished this procession was the sheer number of participants. Of course, the street was blocked off and there were brightly colored lights decorating the yeshiva. A large, colorful vehicle was blaring festive music, and about 3,000 people were walking—many were dancing in front of and around the chuppah—escorting the *Sefer Torah* to its new dwelling place. Hordes of children were milling around and reveling in the festivities. It was fun to watch!

These few weeks, besides my weekly Yiddish club where I enjoy very *geshmak* singing, I am attending a weekly adult education class in Yiddish where we are learning about immigration to the United States and Israel. The class features the teacher reading some charming Sholem Aleichem vignettes, most of which I can understand. I continue to learn weekly, by telephone, with a Yiddish teacher and seem to be making some progress. Additionally, I still subscribe to the weekly newspaper, *Forvitz*, and try to read some of it regularly.

My Hebrew *ulpan* continues to be challenging. One part of the curriculum is listening to the news on the radio. The main obstacle to my comprehension is the speed at which the announcer speaks. We are also reading a captivating novel, A Tale of Love and Darkness by Amos Oz. I attend the *ulpan* twice a week for four hours each session.

Some cultural activities include enjoying a well-done documentary film on Chassidic life in New York, shown at the OU Israel Center, and a wonderful performance of the Israel Philharmonic Orchestra at Binyanei HaUma (the International Conference Center in Jerusalem). Its vast auditorium was filled. I also saw Rimsky-Korsakov's opera *The Golden Cockerel* on a large TV screen at the home of some friends. The performance was introduced by the host, a very talented music maven who won an international contest by listening to classical compositions and identifying them.

As I do my routine early morning Friday rounds, I see primarily men shopping, buying flowers from the Friday vendors and shepherding their young children to school. I'm again reminded that although these Chareidi men receive a small financial stipend from their kollels, where they learn Talmud all day, the main sustenance of the family falls upon the wife. This leads me to another subject: Chareidi women online.

Most of the young wives I know are working in computers. Despite their special requirements —working with women only, flexible hours, and frequent three-month maternity leaves—computer companies are eager to hire them. This is because they accept lower salaries. On this subject, I recently read the following in *The Jerusalem Post*:

> There is a women's professional networking group whose mission statement is "Building Homes and Careers L'Shem Shamayim (for the Sake of Heaven)." This group meets monthly providing an opportunity for its Chareidi members to learn safe ways to evaluate and use the Internet and the new forms of social media. Since observant women are active at every level of the business world, and especially active in the online economy, this network meets a widespread need.

Israel boasts 4,000 computer startups, second in the world only to the United States.

Wednesday, February 24, 2010

After all the time I've spent in Israel, I have not acclimated to the taste of

Jerusalem tap water. Therefore, I drink only the bottled variety. The hard water makes washing dishes an extra effort, and cleaning glassware is quite difficult. Fortunately, I have a *dood shemesh* (solar-powered water tank) on the roof of my building, and because of abundant sunshine most of the year round, the hot water is activated just a few minutes after turning on the faucet.

Jerusalem is gradually becoming "greener." About a year ago, large containers appeared on selected street corners for recycling plastic bottles, and about six months ago, containers for recycling paper were added. I read that there may be some plans soon for recycling cans and glass bottles.

The happy Purim holiday mood is in the air; hamantaschen, masks and baskets for *mishloach manot* abound. In the past few days, I've heard four lectures on the subject of Purim. One was focused on Mordechai and his relationship to the Jewish communities.

Another, in my *ulpan*, included a discussion of a surprisingly long list of expressions from the *Megillah* that are in current usage; for example, Esther's comment to Mordechai when she agrees to risk approaching the king, "*ka'asher ovadeti ovadeti*" (If I am to perish, so be it).

A third speaker stressed that drinking wine is appropriate, since the theme of drinking wine is featured in much of the *Megillah*. Each party is termed a *mishteh*, a drinking occasion. But, says the sage Maimonides, wine should accompany a meal to help stave off total inebriation.

The subject of the fourth lecture was the various opinions on determining which cities in Israel celebrate Purim on the 15th of Adar, Shushan Purim. Jerusalem, which was walled in the days of Joshua, celebrates only Shushan Purim. Included in this discussion was: 1) which suburbs are considered Jerusalem proper and thereby celebrate on the 15th of Adar, and 2) that there are a number of cities in Israel regarding which there is reasonable doubt whether they were walled in Joshua's times. These include the ancient cities of Yaffo, Lod, Akko, Teverya and Chevron, which observe both the 14th and the 15th of Adar. Most of the world celebrates Purim on the 14th of Adar.

People in Israel tend to label themselves, and my friend asked me where I fit into the Orthodox spectrum. I concluded that whereas I'm very comfortable in the Chareidi world, I'm probably more at home with the Modern Orthodox label. Most of my friends in Bayit VeGan are Chareidi, as are my children and their families. While my children all keep the same basic halachot, they each emphasize different *minhagim*. Some examples are: Shira doesn't open sealed bottles on Shabbat, following the Chazon Ish; Rashi stresses proper ethical and moral conduct—for example, no gossiping, as per the Chofetz Chaim; Hillel follows the Lubavitch custom of not decorating his sukkah; and Ronit incorporates the Brisk ritual of keeping Shabbat an additional 40 minutes.

Sunday, April 18, 2010

I have recently returned from a safe, sound and happy trip to London and the United States. Some highlights include the outstanding wedding of my granddaughter Yocheved at which her dad, Rabbi Rashi, officiated. The big event took place with a chuppah and reception in the afternoon, followed by a two-hour hiatus, after which guests returned to a sumptuous dinner and festive celebration. The following week featured strikingly orchestrated *Sheva Brachot* at several homes, each more opulent than the previous. Other highlights were the chance to visit with my California *mechutanim*, enjoying ravishing meals, and being inspired by impressive *divrei Torah*.

In the States, I appreciated the warm welcome of my East Coast family and friends, and of course of my Midwest Lafayette community. I spent Pesach with my daughter Ronit and family in Milwaukee. Among the many guests they hosted was a family from Tashkent, Uzbekistan. I really enjoyed listening to their holiday melodies. In addition to Ronit's delicious cooking, her husband Boruch gave engrossing *divrei Torah* at each meal. At one point, when he began a story about the blood libels in Europe years ago, members of the Tashkent family became very excited and interrupted to say that, although during the year their children had played with the nearby gentile neighbors, around Pesach time the gentile children were forbidden to play with Jewish children—a modern day recurrence of the blood libel.

It has been pleasant to return to my light and sunny Jerusalem apartment. Here, I was greeted with Israeli flags festooned on all the roadside poles in anticipation of Yom HaAtzmaut, also called Chag HaAtzmaut, meaning "Holiday" rather than "Day" of Independence. Many schools are closed and numerous festive events are planned, including Israeli dancing and singing in the public squares. Last week, we commemorated Yom HaShoah when the entire country stood still for two minutes of silence in memory of the Holocaust victims. By the way, in Israel this special memorial day is called

Yom HaShoah Ve-HaGevurah (adding the word "heroism" to the title). Tomorrow is Yom HaZikaron Lechalelei Ma'arachot Yisrael Ulenifgaei Peulot Ha-Eivah, literally, "Remembrance Day for Israel's Fallen Soldiers and Victims of Terrorism." One long program will feature remarks from families who have tragically lost two members in Israel's various wars and enemy encounters. It is also currently the period of the Omer when we count the days from Pesach to Shavuot daily.

I learned about an interesting service that the State of Israel provides to the bereaved parents of soldiers lost in the seven wars in which Israel has had to engage since its inception. A social worker comes to the family's home each year on Yom HaZikaron to listen, comfort and air memories. A friend, who is a bereaved parent, said it was helpful to speak with an understanding person.

Chag HaAtzmaut is a legal holiday, with all businesses as well as almost all schools closed. Chareidi boys have their distinct curriculum. I was able to enjoy a festive dinner with a friend to celebrate the holiday.

I conclude this missive with a warm welcome to my granddaughter Yocheved and her new husband, Yehoshua, who have just arrived from London to begin their married life in Jerusalem.

Friday, April 30, 2010

When I think of the Old City, I realize the tremendous historical and spiritual hold it has upon us. We are reminded that King David walked there and that we are a link in a chain that goes back thousands of years. The colors, smells, narrow streets and architecture give the area enormous charm, so I was quite surprised to read an article in the newspaper *Haaretz*: "Jerusalem's Old City – an Unexpected Haven for Rare Animal and Plant Life."

The author claims that the Old City provides an ecological link between two climate zones – the edge of the desert and the Mediterranean region – and this can be seen in its flora and fauna. "Gardens and orchards thrive amid the crowded quarters on rooftops, while in abandoned areas, old walls, ancient pools and winter rain pools are home to plants, reptiles and birds." One of the rare plants is the Sicilian snapdragon, and "two unexpected avian residents…are the booted eagle and the common quail…. [The Kotel] is home to about 40 nesting pairs of swifts."

Hopefully, some of my friends will come to visit and we can stroll through the Old City as I share these wonderful sights with them.

Friday, May 21, 2010

Lag BaOmer featured the usual bonfires, with the admonition to residents to close their windows, since the air everywhere is smoke-filled. There were elaborate preparations for davening in the caves of the tzaddikim at Meron; for example, over one thousand buses prepared to convey the estimated half a million people expected to travel there. Lag BaOmer in Meron is the traditional time and place for three-year-old boys to get their first haircut.

Recently, at the Jerusalem Theater, I enjoyed a Yiddish musical comedy, a spoof on the Purim *Megillah* titled *Di Megileh fun Itsik Manger*. I also enjoyed some exceptionally pleasant Shabbat invitations. One was to the home of a well-known physicist who recently returned from presenting a paper on superconductivity at a large international conference in Turkey. He said that although the Turks organized and arranged the conference, there wasn't a single Turkish physicist presenting work. He added that the hotel and other prices in general were very inexpensive in Turkey, which may be one of the reasons that it is a favorite Israeli vacation spot.

The past few weeks have included many holidays. I am still learning on which days the secular, Modern Orthodox and Chareidi girls – not boys – have vacation from school and on which days everyone has vacation. Some of these holidays have been inaugurated more recently and their customs are still evolving. Then there is Isru Chag, literally, "bound to the *chag*," which is the day after *Yom Tov* (Pesach, Shavuot and Sukkot) – another day for the holiday atmosphere to linger – when no one has school but all businesses are open. During *chol hamo'ed* there is no school; however, businesses are closed for half a day, some even for the entire day, so it's best to inquire before making shopping plans.

As is common all over on Shavuot, most people studied until about 4:30 a.m. and then davened *Shacharit* before returning home to sleep. I had an unusual opportunity to hear *Megillat Ruth* (customarily read on Shavuot) in Yiddish for the first time. I was reminded of the only Pesach seder that Ed and I spent alone, when we read the Haggadah both in Hebrew and in Yiddish.

Not long ago, I enjoyed an uplifting Shabbat in Lod with my newly married grandson Menachem and his wife, Merav. In addition to reveling in their warm and pampering hospitality, I learned a few facts about the city. Lod is an ancient city comparable to Teverya, Tzfat, and Akko; however, it has no architectural remnants of its thriving eras. This is in contrast to the other ancient cities, which have graves, caves, artifacts and various remains. Lod is 20 percent Arab and has been known for its high crime rate and drug dealing. These problems as well as its very old sewage system, which often springs leaks, are now being addressed. Menachem gives a daily shiur for about 40 minutes in a Sephardic shul, while he davens on Shabbat in his more familiar Ashkenazic shul. I visited both places and commented on how much fancier and attractive the Sephardic shul was than the Ashkenazic. He responded that this is generally the case in Israel.

I learned a little about Jewish genealogy from my upstairs neighbors who hosted me on Shabbat. Both spouses descend from the Sephardim who were evicted from Spain over five hundred years ago. The man's family went to Morocco and retained its Sephardic identity, while the wife's forebears settled in Germany and took on Ashkenazic customs through the years. There are two different strands of customs among the Moroccan Sephardim. One is closer to the Ashkenazic *minhagim* – such as not naming a newborn after a living person. Because of their similar origins the couple found they had a number of customs in common. Incidentally, the wife is descended from the famous Ashkenazic Bamberger family.

Sunday, July 11, 2010

Last week I joined a group of people who accompanied Rabbi Berel Wein on a four-day retreat in the commodious Kibbutz Lavi Hotel, located in the Lower Galilee. The trip featured Rabbi Wein's lectures on the Jews of Russia, France and Germany from 1840 to 1930. He also gave a Shabbat *drasha* and study session on *Pirkei Avot* (Ethics of the Fathers). The rabbi's presentations were eloquent and scholarly. He has set up a foundation called Destiny, which distributes videos – detailing various epochs in Jewish history – to schools and shuls around the world. In addition to the talks, we were feted with sumptuous, fresh and tasty kibbutz meals, treated to views of verdant fields, and we reveled in the fresh mountain air and beguiling Galilee scenery. I should add that the economic base of the kibbutz is its thriving hotel business as well as its Lavi Furniture Industries factory, which designs and produces synagogue and temple furniture, exporting it the world over.

The tours to and from the kibbutz included stops at several wineries, where we learned, for example, that while most barrels for ageing wine come from France and impart certain flavors to the wine, some barrels are bought in America and impart other flavors. There was, of course, sampling at the wineries. We also visited a moshav that raises goats and produces a variety of delectable goat cheese, which we tasted.

Guides along the way delivered detailed data on the areas the bus was traveling. Another amazing stop was at the Ramat Hanadiv Memorial Gardens, a large and verdant area near the town of Zichron Yaakov, which housed the graves of Baron Edmond de Rothschild and his wife. They both died in the early 1930s and were buried in Paris until 1954 when their remains were transported to Israel aboard a naval warship. At the port of Haifa the ship was met with sirens and a 19-gun salute. A state funeral was held with former Prime Minister David Ben-Gurion delivering the eulogy after which Edmond de Rothschild and his wife were re-interred in Ramat Hanadiv. The Baron adopted Israel as one of his beloved causes and spent much of his time and largess in this area of the Galilee. Included in the exquisitely nurtured gardens is a section of special interest, an aromatic herb garden designed with the visually impaired in mind, so that each plant's fragrance could be enjoyed.

I should add that the guide reminded us that the region we traversed is called Binyamin, which belonged to the biblical tribe of Benjamin. The Binyamin neighborhood was also King Saul's territory. We passed *yishuvim* with names such as Migron (a biblical name), Psagot, and Kochav Yaakov. I learned that Nablus, the Arabic word for Shechem, is made up of the Greek words "nea polis" (new city), but there is no "p" sound in Arabic. We saw a large monument to Joshua, which was built because he spent time in an area near the town Elon Moreh. The stones were collected from the paths of his other wanderings, so they gave the monument a feel of authenticity.

At the hotel, we heard a lecture on the New Shomer (Guardian). Over 100 years ago in the Galilee there was a cadre of Jews who protected the Galilee villages, riding around the area on horses. This group no longer exists, but now there is a serious problem with cattle being stolen from Jewish farmers. The thieves operate in the middle of the night, or on Shabbat, and the farmers are worn out from trying to protect their land.

A very new organization has sprung up to give help and support to these harassed farmers. High school graduates who would like to give a year of National Service before entering the army will be housed near the various farms and will guard them. The Keren Kayemet, which helped purchase the land from the Arabs, now needs to encourage more young Jews to buy the land from the older farmers.

We traveled in the part of Israel that belonged to the tribe of Naftali. The city of Tiberias, which ironically is named for the Roman Emporer Tiberius, is now the resting place for many tzaddikim and has become an important center of Torah learning.

Another stop on our tour was Mekorot, a fascinating and highly guarded center for water distribution throughout Israel. Due to strict security, we had to leave all belongings, including purses, on the bus. Some facts I gleaned were that Israel and Spain are the top world leaders in desalinating water. Israel is also beginning to desalinate water from the Mediterranean, and 15 percent of our water should be coming from the sea. The Mekorot Plant we visited is close to the Kinneret and the water is piped from there and from underground aquifers. Israel's methods of water purification and irrigation have attracted researches the world over.

The tour participants were interesting and sociable people, so that all in all I enjoyed a very refreshing, informative and pleasant experience.

Friday, July 23, 2010

This past weekend I was so pleased to have a friend from a small town in Iowa spend a few days with me. Remarkably, she was sponsored by a group in the States that visits small Jewish communities and if they feel there is Jewish leadership potential will underwrite an amazing, fact-filled, three-week stay here for $500. My friend then took a week on her own to explore various sites in Jerusalem including the Bible Lands Museum, the Shrine of the Book, where the Dead Sea Scrolls are housed, the newly renovated Israel Museum, and King David's Citadel. She visited an impressive number of other areas; for example, the Aaronson House Museum in Zichron Yaakov, the Lebanese border, and Beer Sheva. Her tour included Hebrew classes and lectures on a wealth of Jewish topics, such as *Jewish Leadership in the State of Israel and Israeli Society Today*.

Last week I wrote about Mekorot, the central water facility that distributes water throughout Israel. Our group learned that Israel's water, which is checked frequently, is among the very safest in the world. My recent Shabbat host pointed out that a technician comes four times daily to check the reservoir at the end of my street. It services all of Jerusalem, as Bayit VeGan is the second highest spot in the city. Interestingly, the rabbis permit this technician to come in his small truck on Shabbat, despite the fact that our neighborhood is closed to vehicular traffic on that day.

When you arrive at the airport in Israel, you may choose to travel to your specific destination by rental car, private taxi, *sherut*, bus, or to some areas by train. If your destination is Jerusalem, the most popular vehicle seems to be the shuttle, called the *sherut*. It costs around 50 shekel per person and could involve some delays, such as waiting for 10 people to fill up the van and then delivering the passengers to their respective destinations. If you're not too tired and have the time, the plus side is that sometimes you have an unusual tour of Jerusalem and environs.

The car rental has obvious advantages, but the rental place is not very near the airport and you should budget about an hour to take care of all the details. The bus is not advisable for people who are really tired or who have heavy packages. I think the fare is not more than 20 shekel, and it goes to the *Tachana Merkazit* (Central Bus Station in Jerusalem) in Jerusalem. The private taxi costs about 250 shekel and can accommodate up to four passengers. You may get charged a bit extra for large suitcases.

In Jerusalem proper, I prefer that the taxi driver use the meter, and most are very accommodating because that's the law. However, if you know a fair price to your destination and are willing to bargain, you may save some money, since the driver is happy not to use the meter. From 5:30 a.m. to 9:00 p.m. there is a number 1 next to the meter, while from 9:00 p.m. to 5:30 a.m. you will see the number 2, indicating a 25% increase in the fare. The higher fare is also in effect from approximately one hour before Shabbat until 5:30 Sunday morning. There is a 3.60 shekel surcharge for every large suitcase; more than two passengers is an additional 4 shekel, and ordering a taxi increases the price by another 4 shekel. I should add that within the city there is abundant bus transportation available.

The first railway station in Jerusalem, built by the Ottoman Empire, was opened in September 1892, in the area between Hebron Road and Bethlehem Road, near the German Colony. At the time, Eliezer Ben-Yehuda, the man instrumental in the revival of the Hebrew language, coined a new word for train – *rakevet*. In August 1998, the Jerusalem-Tel Aviv line was officially closed but, after being out of service for over six years, it was restored at a new location with the opening of the Malcha Train Station in April 2005. The old, historic station was revived as a center for culture in Jerusalem and is now called the Old Train Station Plaza.

The Jerusalem-Tel Aviv train is noted for its scenery rather than its speed. Journey time from Jerusalem's Malcha Train Station to the center of Tel Aviv is about an hour and a half. In Tel Aviv there are four stops. A high-speed rail link connecting Jerusalem to Tel Aviv in half an hour, and Jerusalem to Ben Gurion Airport in 20 minutes, is under construction and is scheduled to open in 2017. There are many obstacles to overcome, such as the need to build tunnels through the mountains, and bridges over possible archeological finds. Until then, it's best to use the train if you have plenty of time and want to see nice mountain scenery, but not if you are in a hurry.

Monday, August 23, 2010

My grandson Yechiel, from Milwaukee, spent a very happy month participating in an Israeli, Orthodox, English-speaking camp. The staff was mature and competent. The program consisted of davening, learning – generally focusing on the Jewish laws of ethical and moral conduct – the usual sports, of course (stressing soccer, Israel's most popular sport), and many trips to places of interest in the Golan. These *tiyulim* consisted of visits to the holy sites in Tiberias such as the grave of Rabbi Meir Baal HaNess, rappelling, bungee jumping, tubing on the Jordan River, and hiking in the many awesome wadis. A special activity was preparing food boxes for many bereaved families. Tragically, there are constantly new ones. The camp was based in two areas: the first was in the Meah Shearim section of Jerusalem, which is a cultural immersion in itself, and the second segment took place in the majestic mountains of the Golan Heights.

In the summer, it is not uncommon for young girls aged 10 to 16 to organize small *kaytanot* for younger children in their neighborhoods. One such *kaytana* was planned and orchestrated by my 11-year-old granddaughter Chana and her friend. The two girls registered 30 participants, ages 3 to 6, for their well-planned program. They purchased all the supplies, budgeted their resources, charged reasonable fees, and earned a nice profit for themselves. The camp lasted about a week and met daily from 9:00 a.m. to 1:00 p.m.

in my daughter Shira's apartment. I was very impressed by their initiative, entrepreneurship, maturity, and administrative and leadership skills.

Meanwhile, Shira's older boys, 21-year-old Menachem and 18-year-old Mordechai, spent their three-week summer vacation working hard. In addition to organizing first aid courses for yeshiva boys, given by licensed teachers in four or five cities, Menachem taught himself book binding. Several shuls with worn out siddurim and *chumashim* have been paying him to renew their books, so he now has a healthy cottage industry. Mordechai has been delivering fliers in several cities for various companies, advertising their wares. He is a reliable, fast worker and his skills are in demand.

Unfortunately, I have had the recent opportunity to spend a week in Shaarei Tzedek Hospital. I noticed a few differences from my stays in Lafayette hospitals. One distinction is the variety of visitors' garb, denoting various segments of the Jewish and Arab communities. Another is the fact that a patient's general physician is not allowed in the hospital. The hospital physicians do not have any contact with the patient's primary healthcare provider. I was seen by a different doctor each day. Although the care seems adequate, I feel it is important to have an ombudsman nearby to get information that is not readily forthcoming. I was very fortunate to have had my daughter Shira come daily to help clarify various points. Since Shaarei Tzedek is very near my home, I had many visitors, including doting neighbors.

The hospital building is modern and the rooms are pleasant and commodious, though private rooms are non-existent. I was surprised that telephone, TV and Internet have to be ordered and paid for privately. On the other hand, there should be no charge for the hospital stay. We'll see. I've been primarily speaking Hebrew, as many of the medical personnel are Russian and speak only a limited amount of English, if at all. I learned three new medical terms: *balutot lympha* are lymph nodes; *manjeta* is the arm cuff used for measuring blood pressure; and EKG is pronounced *eh - keh - geh* (hard "g"). Shaarei Tzedek is an Orthodox hospital, though as far as I know, kosher food is served in all of Israel's hospitals.

An only-in-Israel occurrence happened to one of my visitors. As she was exiting the hospital on Shabbat, planning to walk home, an Orthodox woman who was visiting another patient invited her to spend Shabbat at her nearby home, thinking that my friend might have to walk a long distance.

On an entirely different hospital subject, my daughter Shira who works as a doula, or birth coach, told me that most hospitals allow only a two-night stay to women giving birth. There are two Orthodox hospitals that allow three nights. However, if a mother is willing to go home after two nights, she can get a small cash bribe. One hospital allows more than three nights to women who have already given birth to at least seven children. In conclusion, I am feeling fine and emerged from my hospital experience with a clean bill of health, *Baruch Hashem*.

Monday, September 13, 2010

My friend and her family moved recently to their own apartment. *Shiputzim* (renovations) is a frequently used term here. Usually one hires a Jewish contractor, called a *kablan*, who employs Arab workers to do the renovations. My friend visited her new abode several times daily before moving in, to check on the progress of the work. She noticed that the employees were working very slowly. The air conditioner hadn't yet been installed, so she proffered some glasses of water, but they were refused. Observing Ramadan requires daily fasting from dawn to sunset. The workers left by 3:30 p.m.

Rosh HaShanah has just passed, and as the new year commences I would like to describe my week's program:

Sunday and Tuesday mornings I attend an *ulpan* where we read the newspaper, listen to the news on the radio and read various texts by Haim Sabato, Meir Shalev, S.Y. Agnon, and Amos Oz, all contemporary Israeli authors. It is demanding, and the other adults seem very bright. In addition, Yiddish is tripping off my tongue as I chat with my private Yiddish teacher once a week by phone. I also read several texts in that language. A weekly treat is my Yiddish club, which features fascinating lecturers and very talented actors, singers, musicians, and more. It is really fun! In addition, I have a friend who knows Yiddish better than I and has a very sweet singing voice. She comes here weekly and we sing Yiddish songs together. We even presented a program for a local women's group, Emunah, based on the program I gave for the Lafayette Yiddishe Kultur Vinkel.

My Monday morning *shiur* takes place in a central Jerusalem neighborhood and attracts about 150 English-speaking women. We learn fascinating insights on the *Tanach* from each of two very capable women lecturers.

On Wednesday morning, I join about eight or nine neighborhood women in a shiur given by a learned rabbi on Jewish laws pertaining to the upcoming holidays, questions of kashrut, or other topics. This rabbi also teaches at various girls' seminaries.

My piano skills are maintained by continuing twice weekly to play duets with my partner of 35 years. In addition, I accompany a flautist and a violinist and am teaching another pianist to play duets. Eventually, I hope they will play together in a very amateur klezmer ensemble. We'll see!

Once a month I travel close to an hour each way to Ramat HaSharon to play recorder with a group of about 10 recorder teachers. We play soprano, alto, tenor and bass recorders. Recorder, or *chalilit*, is a mandatory subject in many schools, so it is very popular here.

On Shabbat afternoon, I regularly attend a talk on the weekly Torah portion, given each time by a different eminent rabbi. This *shiur* attracts about 50 English-speaking women in my neighborhood. In a sense, my neighborhood is like an academic community, since almost every building houses at least one or two learned rabbis. So, there are enough speakers within a few blocks to have each rabbi lecture only once, or maybe twice a year.

A major project dear to my heart is editing Ed's thousands of papers with my talented granddaughter, the newly married Yocheved.

I should add that socially, I've been invited by friends and neighbors for almost every Shabbat meal since I've arrived. Also, my guest room has been occupied by family and friends about 50 percent of the time.

Comparing my current activities with those during my 45 years in Lafayette, I would say there has been continuity of some themes: study groups on Jewish topics, improving my Hebrew and Yiddish language skills, playing recorder and piano with partners, teaching some piano lessons, and organizing an Israeli klezmer ensemble. However, in contrast, here I attend lectures by various rabbis on Jewish topics, do not teach Hebrew to youngsters, and do not bake and sell challot, hamantaschen and other baked goods. I do not preside over Hadassah and the Sons of Abraham Sisterhood, nor do I do much volunteer work. But in Israel I can spend quality time with my family, including interacting often with my three married grandchildren. My teenage grandsons from London and the United States are studying in yeshivot here and visit frequently. Israel's proximity to London is a plus. Also, living in the Holy City of Jerusalem has afforded me many opportunities for spiritual, social, cultural and intellectual growth in my quest for *shleimut* (wholeness) in my relationship to *Hashem*. A tremendous benefit is living with my people in the land given to us by G-d, where the past comes alive, the present is multilayered and challenging, and I can be part of its destiny.

Thursday, October 07, 2010

The people of Israel greatly admire and appreciate those young men and women from the world over who come on their own to serve in the Israeli armed forces. These "lone soldiers" are invited to homes for the holidays when they are granted a *chamshush* – an extended leave for **cham***ishi*-Thursday, **shi***shi*-Friday, and **Sh**abbat. In addition, they are sent gifts of food, toiletries and other amenities, by volunteer organizations. Tragically, some of these lone soldiers fell in the 1973 Yom Kippur War. Each year before Yom Kippur, a charitable woman notes the names of these soldiers as inscribed on their gravestones and organizes a minyan for the day after Yom Kippur to say *Kaddish* in their memory. My grandson Simcha, who is spending the year learning in a nearby yeshiva, participated recently with nine other boys from his yeshiva in several *Kaddish* minyanim at the military cemetery. Simcha just graduated with high honors in advanced math and physics from his Jewish high school in London.

I spent the Yamim Noraim with my sons' families in London. Services at Rashi's shul, on Rosh HaShanah and Yom Kippur, segued seamlessly. The davening was punctuated by Rabbi Rashi's elevating and enlightening remarks; the atmosphere was spiritually charged. I was comfortable, welcomed, and uplifted by my participation in the services. Similarly, Ruthie's lavish, tasty, healthful and abundant holiday and Shabbat meals were a gustatory delight. The intermediate days were spent in a restful, *nachesdig* and restorative atmosphere at Hillel and Yael's very hospitable home.

Immediately upon my return to Israel after Yom Kippur, my grandson Menachem and his wife, Merav, came to build and decorate my sukkah. They then spent the week here, which culminated in the arrival of my sister-in-law Harriet and her grandson Caleb, who is also studying in a nearby yeshiva this year. Ronit came from Milwaukee with her two daughters, and we enjoyed her excellent cooking for the holidays and Shabbat, ably aided by Harriet. Of course, the holiday atmosphere here, including festive attire, music and dancing, is most beguiling. Hillel and two of his sons, as well as Rashi and Ruthie, arrived after Sukkot to participate in our memorial seminar and visit Ed's grave just after his fourth *yahrtzeit*. All told, we saw 27 people around my dining area table who conducted a most memorable hour-long seminar. Each person read a short segment from the vast collection of Ed's letters. Shira had compiled a 31-page booklet with many of Ed's favorite aphorisms and songs, and he "came alive." After davening at his gravesite, which commands a spectacular view of a wide swath of Jerusalem and environs, we were transported to an upscale restaurant for more memories and socializing.

Thursday, October 14, 2010

We spent last Shabbat at the Kibbutz Lavi Hotel reveling in a restorative, refreshing, and relaxing celebration of my birthday, thus concluding the week of a meaningful visit here by Rashi and his family. On the two-hour drive up north, we unexpectedly traveled in Israel's first rain of the season, which lasted about 10 minutes, and were then treated to the sight of a large and rare rainbow. Amazingly, this occurred during the week of the Shabbat portion of *Noach*. The kibbutz meals featured a plethora of fresh produce. As the kibbutz is situated in the Lower Galilee, we enjoyed a scenic walking tour during which the guide pointed out several historical sites, such as: the Jezreel Valley, where Barak (commander of the army of Devorah, the prophetess and judge) fought and defeated the Canaanite armies led by Sisera [Judges: chap. 4]; the spring of Harod, where Gideon the Judge led only 300 Israelites in successful battle against the Midianites and Amalekites [Judges: chap. 6-8]; and Mount Gilboa, where King Saul later lost his life fighting the Philistines [1 Samuel: chap. 14].

Thursday, October 28, 2010

My *mechutan* Dr. Reading Dallal very sadly died several weeks ago. He was well known and influential in the Evanston/Skokie Jewish community. Reading was head of the Hebrew Department at Evanston High School and was a skillful, innovative teacher there for many years. A warm, creative and charming man, he also taught Hebrew and Arabic (which he learned in Israel and in his native Iraq) at DePaul University in Chicago. Reading published a book about the life of the Jews in Iraq, and he tried to communicate his heritage to his grandchildren. He leaves his wife, three children including my daughter-in-law Yael, and 15 grandchildren.

On another note, I recently learned two new words in Hebrew. The color brown is *chum*, and brownies are *chumiyot*. Cranberries (which I've never seen fresh here), because of their tart taste, are called *chamutziot* derived from the word *chometz*, vinegar.

I learned that on Rachel Imeinu's *yahrtzeit*, the 11th of Cheshvan, almost 100,000 people came to pray at her *kever* and that although the Egged bus company had prepared a constant stream of buses, the immense crowds were difficult to handle. Biblical scholars had some differences of opinion as to the precise location of Rachel's *kever*, but they finally agreed that the present site is valid. It is about a 20-minute trip from Jerusalem, on the road to Bethlehem. According to ancient tradition, a red string that has been wound seven times around Rachel's *kever* is endowed with mystical powers. By tying the string (or a piece of it) around his or her wrist, the wearer is protected from the destructive power of the evil eye. A friend wore one of these wrist bands for a long time, believing it to be a good omen for prayers to be answered.

The 15th *yahrtzeit* of Yitzchak Rabin's death falls the next day, on the 12th of Cheshvan, and his *kever* is located on Mount Herzl, which has served as Israel's national cemetery since 1951. It is the burial place of three of Israel's prime ministers: Levi Eshkol, Golda Meir and Yitzchak Rabin (who is interred beside his wife, Leah). Israeli presidents are also buried on Mount Herzl, as are other prominent Jewish and Zionist leaders. Mount Herzl is the venue for many commemorative events and national celebrations and is not too far from my apartment. Every year, Yitzchak Rabin's daughter and various dignitaries speak at the commemoration ceremony on his *yahrtzeit*. May his memory be for a blessing.

Monday, November 15, 2010

When a Jewish girl turns 12, she becomes obligated to observe all the commandments of the Torah, and is therefore a full-fledged bat mitzvah. As far as I know there is a wide variety of rituals celebrating a girl's bat mitzvah. I believe the custom of making a party was initiated about 60 years ago. Having grown up in Conservative religious circles, I knew no one who had a bat mitzvah party. The rite of passage was the Sweet 16 party. I recently had the chance to participate in my granddaughter Chana's special event. The occasion was commemorated on her Hebrew 12th birthday, which is typical in religious circles. In many schools the girls are not allowed to invite any of their classmates to the celebration, the reason being that the classes are large, 35-40 students, and most girls will turn 12 during the same year. A bat mitzvah girl would generally invite the entire class and that would cost a lot of money. In addition, the school prepares a big production with all the girls in the bat mitzvah-age class.

My daughter Shira planned a charming afternoon celebration. About 18 guests came, including Chana's older sister, sister-in-law, aunt, cousins, neighbors, and family friends. The program was creative, entertaining and inspiring. Chana gave an eloquent speech, thanking in detail all her relatives and expressing her feelings upon assuming the role of adulthood. One of the neighbors gave a stirring *d'var Torah*, mentioning that now that Chana was bat mitzvah her prayers would be included in those of all the congregation of the Jewish people. Chana and her younger sister Mirale performed some original dances, and there was spontaneous singing as I played some festive music of Chana's favorite songs on the keyboard. Challah dough was brought in and, now that she was bat mitzvah and therefore considered an adult in Jewish law, Chana was able to fulfill the important commandment of separating a portion of the challah dough. For the first time, she made the blessing on "taking challah," which was followed by a heartfelt prayer. In Temple times, the dough would be gifted to the *kohanim* (priests).

The next day, Chana and her mom came up to Jerusalem to pray at the Kotel, then met me and a cousin for lunch. A piece of gold jewelry is a traditional gift for a bat mitzvah, and Chana's parents presented her with a pretty gold necklace.

Sunday, December 5, 2010

On Sunday evenings I attend a lecture combined with music on the *parshah* of the week. Last Sunday, I especially enjoyed the talk on the role of shepherds in our nation's history – Jacob, Moses, and others. The speaker quoted from a Ph.D. thesis on this subject. In addition, there are a number of lovely songs about shepherds – in particular, an especially prayerful song by Naomi Shemer, "Shirat Ha'asavim." The singer's rendition was riveting. Years ago, storytellers, *magidim*, would wander from village to village, preaching and telling stories for purposes of instruction and repentance. They would often embellish their tales with chant-like music lines. These chants were included in this very popular song with an additional Naomi Shemer touch. I also learned that the well-known "Hava Nagila" melody was originally sung as a *nigun* and composed by the Sadigura Chassidim.

I'm attending three weddings in six days, a record for me. One of the weddings is a second marriage for the *chatan* and the *kallah*, a widower and widow. I learned several new customs pertaining to second marriages. The children of the *chatan* and *kallah* do not come to the *chuppah*, though they may arrive at the celebration later. The bride circles the groom three times, rather than seven as at a first wedding. Also, just as at a first marriage, *Sheva Brachot* are said under the *chuppah* and again at the end of the festive wedding *seudah*; however, in this case, there are only three days of celebration following the wedding, not seven. According to some opinions, only the blessing of "Asher Bara" – not all seven blessings – may be recited at meals during these three days. This bride has one daughter, who at age 36 has 10 children. The groom has 10 children, 9 of whom are married with young families. The wedding was small – about 60 people – in contrast to most B'nei Brak weddings, which include numbers well into the hundreds. My son-in-law Shlomo pointed out that there is a small street in B'nei Brak in which there are 10 wedding halls – in some cases 2 or 3 in the same building – in which 10 weddings take place nightly. Shlomo added that the street is filled with hired buses, used to transport the many, many guests.

Another wedding was in the nearby town of Beit Shemesh. It was a lively, happy affair. The *kallah's* parents are from Chicago, and on the bus that was chartered by the family to transport the guests, I made a new friend who recently made aliyah from there. As usual, with Jewish geography, we knew a number of people in common.

The following week, I was pleased to have a chance to participate in a guided tour of the newly renovated Israel Museum. The exhibits were elegantly appointed, really state of the art. We visited the galleries of Stone Age items, millions of years old; pottery, thousands of years old; then, many choice items in the hundreds-of-years-old category including the oldest Haggadah, from the thirteenth century. It occurred to me how my late husband, Ed, would have enjoyed seeing this remarkable book. He had amassed about 2,500 varied and interesting Haggadot, including Braille, feminist, and vegetarian versions, as well as those translated into many languages. Ed become an expert on the section of The Four Sons and, thanks to the Purdue Jewish Studies Department, showed slides illustrating his many lectures on that specific topic. When he had duplicate Haggadot, he would trade with several pen pals in various parts of the world. Ed's collection grew in a number of ways: Many friends and relatives gave him Haggadot they no longer used; his children knew what to present him with for each birthday and other special occasions; our son-in-law Shlomo regularly searched the *genizah* (a storage area for holy books that are worn out) in B'nei Brak and found some treasures there; and finally, Ed wrote hundreds of articles for several Jewish newspapers reviewing the newly published Haggadot, and in return for each article he would receive a Haggadah gratis. The collection is now beautifully displayed in Hillel and Yael's home in London. Hillel periodically adds to the collection.

To return to the museum: an especially outstanding exhibit consists of five shuls, which have been transferred, some in total, to the museum. I recollect seeing one from pre-war Berlin, others from Spain, India and Italy, and the latest shul is from Surinam. There is a gift shop and several kosher restaurants, milchig or fleishig, on the premises. A friend of mine remarked after he had visited the museum, "A person could easily spend a week there."

My fledgling klezmer ensemble has been practicing Chanukah songs and we are preparing for a party and a performance. We have five members including a singer, and we are having fun!

An interesting Chanukah sight in my neighborhood is an occasional tall, empty bookcase and shelves covered with aluminum foil. Since it is customary to light *chanukiyot* outside, these shelves feature many, all filled with oil. They are in front of the yeshivot, where each *bachur* (young unmarried man) lights his *chanukiyah*. Apparently, in certain circles, oil is de rigueur. The prominent Chanukah delicacy here is *sufganiyot*. I read a survey in *The Jerusalem Post* in which the *sufganiyot* in eight bakeries were rated for various factors. *Sfog*, in Hebrew, is "a sponge," and *sofeg* means "absorbs." *Sufganiyot* are fried in and absorb a lot of oil.

Chanukah Sameach!

Wednesday, December 15, 2010

I recently heard a lecture at my Rosh Chodesh group, based partly on the book *Start-Up Nation* by Dan Senor and Saul Singer. We learned some facts,

which I cannot verify, such as the following:
- Every cell phone in the world has a microchip developed in Israel.
- There's a law in the Knesset obligating fashion models to pass a weight test so that they avoid anorexia and bulimia.
- Israel is producing innovative hearing aids.
- Scientists are working on a simple blood test to diagnose some forms of cancer.
- Israel, in conjunction with scientists at Harvard, developed an injection to combat macular degeneration.
- On the train ride from Modiin to Tel Aviv, weekly courses are offered. (I don't know in what subjects.)
- Drip irrigation designed by Israel is used in many countries.
- *Forbes* magazine lists Israel as the 22nd best place to live.
- Bill Gates of Microsoft announced "The brains of this company are in Haifa."
- The CAT scan (also known as CT scan) and MRI tests were developed in Israel.

These all highlight Israel's technological contributions to the world.

As we have an abundance of sunlight all year round, solar heating is very common here, but it necessitates a short wait until the cold water is replaced by the heated water. Since there is a great awareness of the importance of conserving water, many families keep a bucket under the shower to collect the initial cold water and then use it for doing *sponja* (washing floors), watering plants, and other household chores. As there's been a real drought, there is a desperate need for rain here, so the rabbis, in addition to adding more prayers at the Kotel and during the daily davening, have declared a fast day. I read that it's been 50 years since the month of November did not have even a drop of rain. There was almost no rain in October and very little since Pesach.

Chapter 4

2011

Tuesday, January 4, 2011

A month ago, a fire blazed out of control in the Carmel Forest near Haifa. We are still empathizing with the people in the northern part of the country who have been so radically affected by the horrific fire. During the past month, when groups got together in various places, people rose to dedicate a few moments of silence in memory of the 43 fatalities. I read just last week that the 44th burn victim had died. *Baruch Dayan HaEmet*.

As I've mentioned, one of my cultural activities is attending a weekly lecture and demonstration connecting the Torah portion with music. Recently, a well-known composer sang several of his popular songs. I thought of the contrast between these titles and some popular songs in the United States, such as Lady Gaga's "Bad Romance" and Eminem's "Love the Way You Lie." Ehud Banai sang his compositions "Ir Miklat" (city of refuge) and "Daveed ve-Shaul" (David and Saul).

I recently read, with more than passing interest, an article about the Hula Nature Reserve in the Galilee, which is a paradise for birds and heaven for bird watchers. I thought how Ed would have enjoyed visiting the thousands of European cranes who have turned the reserve into their year-round home. Ed, in his youth, was an avid bird watcher. In his later years, he decorated our sukkah with many figures of birds, which visitors took delight in identifying. The nature reserve has long been a resting spot for migrating birds traveling from Europe to Africa and Asia, but the cranes, by establishing it as their year-round home, have made the area so noteworthy that in 2009, the magazine *BBC Wildlife* listed it as the number 9 spot out of the top 20 outstanding sites in the world for nature observation. One can see up to 45 species of birds, including cormorants, egrets, pelicans, ibis, herons and eagles.

Friday, January 14, 2011

Not long ago, I had an opportunity to visit Ed's grave. After a very brief survey, I suspect that Ed's is the only gravestone that puts West Lafayette on the Jerusalem map. Interestingly, I learned that each traditional community, such as secular, Sephardic, Ashkenazic and Chareidi, utilizes its own section of the cemetery. A term that was clarified for me is *levaya*, which literally means "escorting" and refers to the funeral procession to the gravesite. In Jerusalem, generally, a corpse may not be left unburied overnight. Thus, the *taharah* (ritual cleansing of the body) and burial are carried out immediately. My grandson Simcha had the experience of being part of four busloads of boys from his yeshiva who, upon arrival at the gate of the cemetery, accompanied the body of his *rosh yeshiva's* mother, by foot, to her gravesite. She had died only a few hours earlier. Another custom new to me is that in many Jewish cemeteries, it is standard procedure not to bury a woman next to any man other than her husband. Therefore, the graves alternate – husband, wife, wife, husband, husband wife, and so on.

I've been attending a number of cultural events in the last few weeks: several concerts, including a piano, cello, clarinet trio; a Yiddish play at the Jerusalem Theater entitled *A Shayna Maidel* ("A Pretty Girl"); a Yiddish concert by two *chazanim* at my Yiddish club; a Verdi opera in Tel Aviv, and more. This week I have a wedding of my close neighbor's sister, in B'nei Brak, as well as a Tu B'Shvat invitation from my grandchildren Menachem and Merav for a meal at their new apartment in B'nei Brak.

My lunch meals are often in various restaurants with friends. By the way, there may be a hundred or more kosher restaurants, cafes and other eateries in Jerusalem, but it is important for many people to know the exact details of the *hechsher* at the restaurant of their choice.

Tuesday, February 01, 2011

For the last six weeks, with a few exceptions, my guest room has been in use. Many of the occupants are from the States, and it seems as though most have a child spending a year in Israel, learning in a yeshiva or seminary after high school graduation. Having friends and family here is an enriching experience for me on several levels. Though it's helpful for visitors to have a comfortable, welcoming place to stay, the relationship is really symbiotic. I don't enjoy living alone and relish the chance to have a more flexible outlook on life. Mainly, I continue my usual activities, and with two small restaurants a few steps away, and a convenient grocery and green grocer nearby, my guests seem to manage. Since most have never lived in Israel, I have a chance to give an occasional suggestion regarding transportation and some advice from my experience of having patronized more than 20 Jerusalem restaurants.

A lingerie store, newly opened in the Geula neighborhood to serve the Chareidi women's community there, has a sign outside stating "No Men Allowed."

I recently learned from a friend that his son-in-law had to be brought to the hospital emergency room in Petach Tikva just before Shabbat. As he was released a few hours later, the staff kindly rounded up an Arab driver who conveyed him back to his *yishuv* and then returned after Shabbat to be compensated. Nice cooperation here! My friend stressed the fact that by far the majority of Jewish and Arab communities here relate well to each other. I imagine my readers sense this from my various letters. I realize the news in the States focuses mostly on politics and occasional, very sad occurrences.

Some news you may have missed: "Israel's agricultural produce companies say they developed some 65 new species of peppers in 2010. Some of the species were displayed at an exhibition on Tu B'Shvat....others will be available in the marketplace during the coming year. These new species are immune to viruses, grow abundantly and are outstanding in their export potential" [*Hamodia* newspaper]. Another *Hamodia* tidbit: "...a pod of 15 dolphins was spotted off the coast of Tel Aviv...a now not uncommon sight that has led experts to conclude that the sea mammals have taken up permanent residence near Israel's shores. 'We believe there are between 300 and 400 Mediterranean bottlenose dolphins...,' the chairman of the research center said." Thus, the headline: "Tel Aviv Becoming a Dolphin

Spotter's Paradise."

We have been blessed with almost a week of occasional rainfall. What I especially enjoy is the feel of the air after the rain. The breeze is so fresh, clean, soft and gentle.

The face of Jerusalem has changed. In particular, the main artery, Jaffa Street, has been closed to vehicular traffic from City Hall to the Machaneh Yehudah market. The closure has engendered some major traffic tie-ups, especially with buses. So far, I've not heard anything positive about the advent of the light rail. It is costing three times the original estimate to build and is close to three years behind schedule for the anticipated functioning date. Nevertheless, I am keeping an open mind to see what actually happens in August. There are pretty saplings planted on the outside of the rails, at least on nearby Herzl Boulevard.

FRIDAY, FEBRUARY 4, 2011

Today, we marked Rosh Chodesh Adar 1 on the Jewish calendar. I was reminded that a leap year is called *shanah meuberet* – literally, "a pregnant year" – because there will also be a second Adar.

After speaking with a friend and testing the expression on my family, I learned a new Hebrew saying. When a person unexpectedly meets someone twice within a short period of time, one of them says *pa'am shlishit, glidah*, meaning "the third time we meet, (you buy me) ice cream." The etiology of the phrase comes from England, where the expression is "the third time, I scream." The Israelis heard "ice cream," therefore the interesting transfer.

SUNDAY, FEBRUARY 13, 2011

Through the years, on my frequent visits here, I always made a point of dipping in the Dead Sea and enjoying the adjacent Ein Gedi Spa. Recently, I have found the stones too slippery to maintain my balance. During my visit to a hotel at the Dead Sea, shortly after my aliyah (close to four years ago), I had to content myself with the Dead Sea water pool within the hotel.

Now, several years later, I'm en route to the Crowne Plaza Hotel at the sea for a three-day Yiddish Festival. I thought some of my friends and family might like to accompany me on a little tour as my bus travels from one of

Israel's four climatic areas to another.

Our bus passes the Inn of the Good Samaritan, army bases, and some construction sites, with the hilly scenery portraying the gradual transition from trees to shrubs to dry, brown-and-red-colored sand. We pass scattered Bedouin encampments along the way. Near these encampments are herds of sheep and goats grazing on the faint greenery covering the red rock mountains. High above us is the Jewish town of Ma'aleh Adumim, literally, "Red Ascent." It takes its name from the red rock lining the ascent from the Dead Sea.

We just passed the sign saying "Sea Level"; nearby, an Arab and a camel stand, I imagine awaiting photo-ops. Israel is famed for several wonders of the world. I know, for example, that Kibbutz Ein Gedi is the only botanical garden in which people reside; and the Dead Sea, known for its palliative qualities, is the lowest place on earth. We pass a rare gas station and a whole row of plant hothouses. We see barren sand hills and wadis with a sparse amount of greenery from the recent rainfall. We turn away from the King Hussein Bridge (known by Israelis as the Allenby Bridge) leading to Jericho as we traverse near rows of small saplings and now increased greenery, including columns of date palm trees, probably watered from a nearby spring or oasis. We pass Qumran, the caves where the Dead Sea Scrolls were originally found. The scrolls are now housed in The Shrine of the Book, a wing of the Israel Museum. We can see the Dead Sea in the distance. The hills have become mountains, crags with very stark, jagged tops, full of stones, caves, and brown-red sand. We are now nearing the turquoise-colored sea reflecting the cloudy sky above. Clearly, in the distance, rise the mountains of Jordan.

There has been very little traffic along the way, probably because the tourist season is over. I read that this year's number of visitors has been the best ever for Israel. Since tourism is one of Israel's top industries, the economy has been greatly strengthened by the influx of tourists. We are passing the Ein Gedi Field School, the Ein Gedi Youth Hostel and Guest House, and the thriving Kibbutz Ein Gedi, which is an oasis sustained by a wonderful mountain spring. Our bus has arrived at a row of four hotels close to the sea, stopping at our five-star Crowne Plaza Hotel, the only one directly on the beach. I am with a group of people from Jerusalem, joining another five busloads of guests from various places in Israel. We will be spending 3 ½ days here at the Yiddish Festival.

Wednesday, February 16, 2011

The well-organized and enjoyable festival program was of a high caliber with talented singers, *chazanim*, actors, klezmer musicians and raconteurs, using Yiddish as the primary language. Over 500 people from a number of major cities participated. In the main, probably most were over 55 years old. The audiences were very responsive, often clapping along with the music and singing familiar songs with the entertainers. There were slides available with words to the songs. Some lectures I found especially interesting were on Marc Chagall's paintings, on I.B. Singer's depictions of shtetl life, and on learning the history of klezmer music through slides of famous artists.

My hotel room included a private porch with a beguiling view of the sea. In the evening, I could see the lights in Jordan across the water; in the day, the calm azure sea reflected clearly the pink, cotton-candy-like, cumulus clouds in the sky. In the dining room, it was fun to taste the *kasha, kreplach,* stuffed grape leaves, and *p'tcha.* The hotel staff was accommodating and the floor plan was convenient, leading easily from the lecture halls to the dining room to the spa, where I indulged in a massage and mud rub. All in all, the experience was positive and memorable.

Thursday, February 17, 2011

If you look at your Jewish calendar on Friday, February 18, which is the 14th of Adar I, you should see the words Purim Katan. If there had been only one Adar this year, that day would have been Purim. However, since this is a leap year, we have two Adars and Purim is observed in the second one. It's been suggested that we should commemorate Purim Katan ("Little Purim") in the first Adar by being especially happy and, for example, enhancing a meal with an extra treat. Happy Purim Katan!

By the way, Jerusalemites commemorate Shushan Purim Katan, since we celebrate Purim on the 15th of Adar.

Thursday, March 17, 2011

This week, following the tragic news of the devastating tsunami in Japan, we are mourning our own tragic terrorist attack and murder of a family of five in the *yishuv* of Itamar. All of Israel is greatly shocked and saddened by the news of this horrific event. The family was buried in Jerusalem, and all traffic was at a standstill for several hours, as many thousands of people accompanied the biers. Two days later, the entire country stood in silence at 11:00 a.m. joining in the pain of the family whose son Gilad Shalit has been held captive in enemy hands for over five years.

However, our Sages say, *Mishenichnas Adar, marbim b'simcha* – When the Hebrew month of Adar enters, joy is increased [Tractate *Megillah*]. Purim is coming, and we are enjoined to be happy. I have heard at least three lectures on various commentaries on *Megillat Esther*. I also learned a clarification of the contents of mishloach manot. It is customary to include two items requiring different *brachot*—for example, one baked food item and a beverage, preferably wine or grape juice—since these can be used for the Purim *seudah*, the traditional meal. In addition to sending at least two gifts of food to one another and eating the festive meal, the other requirements for Purim include listening to the *Megillah* and giving *matanot l'evyonim*.

This Purim my family has an extra special personal reason to celebrate. The *brit mila* of my second great-grandson is scheduled to take place on Purim morning. Shira and Shlomo's eldest daughter, Tovah, gave birth to her second son. We are very grateful and happy. Although Tovah lives in a small town called Kiryat Sefer, or Modi'in Illit, she chose to give birth in Shaarei Tzedek Hospital, about five minutes ride from my house. I found Tovah glowing and I was thrilled to hold the half-day-old infant in my arms. I shall travel to B'nei Brak for the *brit* on their Purim, remaining for the family seudah, then returning with my younger granddaughters to Yerushalayim for our Shushan Purim celebration. They are coming to deliver my *mishloach manot* in the neighborhood and we are invited to my neighbors' *seudah*, which will be held in a hall since that's the best venue for their family of 14 children, 13 of whom are married with families.

Sunday, March 27, 2011

I have recently read the book *Tales out of Jerusalem* by Rabbi Emanuel Feldman, a leading Orthodox rabbi for many years in Atlanta, Georgia. He and his family have resided in Bayit VeGan for over 10 years.

Rabbi Feldman expresses so eloquently many of the reasons I've chosen to live in Jerusalem:

I will try to avoid the usual platitudes about Israel.Yes, it is true that we have sun most of the year, and Jerusalem is breathtaking in its stark beauty, and the Land is filled with an endless variety of people and cultures, and we have mountains and deserts and sea....the religious imperatives of dwelling in the Land that, according to some decisors, actually have the force of a mitzvah....we are not sitting passively in the grandstand while history is being played out before us. Here we have an acute sense of being part of our ancient people, a sense of revisiting the days of yore....

Kedushah [holiness] is endemic in Jerusalem even in the twenty-first century. Let me, ever so briefly, count the ways:

In the synagogues, where davening is of a sincerity and ardor that is not found anywhere; in the study halls, where Torah at all levels is studied by men and women of all intellectual and economic strata, seven days a week, morning, noon and night; in the acts of chesed that are the hallmarks of the Orthodox community - the welcoming of strangers to one's home for Shabbos; the many free-loan societies; the organizations that supply the homebound, the sick and the infirm with food, friendship and encouragement; the care with which religious Jews observe the restrictions against making unfavorable comments about others; the high percentage of their incomes that religious Jews give to tzedakah - in all this, the sense of kedushah is pervasive.While such things are found in most Orthodox communities, the quantity, quality and intensity with which it is manifested in Jerusalem is unmatched anywhere. My own neighborhood of Bayit Vegan, for example, with a population of less than six thousand families, offers - in addition to its fifty chesed groups and sixty synagogues - almost 200 shiurim for adults per week....Even non-religious Jews sense it. My secular taxi driver, rounding a curve that reveals the rolling hills in the distance, exclaims:"Ein kemo Yerushalayim" (There is nothing like Jerusalem). Jerusalem is breathtaking physically; spiritually, it is even more striking.

But there is more. The Jewish soul is attached to the Holy Land by an umbilical cord that extends back to the Patriarchs and to God's promise to them to give us the Land as an inheritance. Upon its every grain of sand rests the imprint of God. "The eyes of God are upon it [Israel] from the beginning of the year until the end of the year," says the Torah in Deuteronomy 11:12. Israel is thus unlike any other land. This is the

dwelling place of the Shechinah, the Presence of G-d. That is why in this place alone, the Jewish soul is fully nourished and at peace.
[*Tales out of Jerusalem,* pp. 272-274]

Although our Purim celebration was joyful, the two months of Adar were marred by the murders in the town of Itamar, as well as a bomb explosion opposite the Jerusalem Central Bus Station, which took the life of one person and injured 40 others. These horrific terrorist attacks affected the mood of the country.

Pesach is in the air, and everyone I talk to has already made his/her *Yom Tov* plans. It is traditional here, as in the world over, for Jews to sell their *chametz* by giving a donation to a rabbi or community leader, who then sells it to a non-Jew. However, there is an additional safeguard in place in Israel. The Chief Rabbis take responsibility to sell the *chametz* for every Jew in the land. This is necessary, I learned, because some stores may not have sold their *chametz* individually, and even after Pesach it is forbidden to derive benefit from *chametz* owned by a Jew during Pesach.

WEDNESDAY, APRIL 6, 2011

I never cease to be amazed by the many acts of *chesed* here. I recently learned of a wonderful project by the people of the small town of Chashmonaim. It is an upscale village of mainly Modern Orthodox families, located about halfway between B'nei Brak and Jerusalem. Thirty families have banded together to provide the soldiers at the checkpoints, nightly, with hot chocolate, coffee, and cold drinks, along with some *nosherai* (snack foods) and an extra treat. Each family takes responsibility for one night of the month, while the remaining families all contribute some items to the person who will be delivering these goodies to the soldiers. The brave young men are so grateful for the warmth, caring and sustenance of these personal visits.

WEDNESDAY, APRIL 13, 2011

As I was walking to the dentist nearby, I noted some unusual sights. First, I saw an empty parking lot filled with hundreds of large trays of eggs and huge canvas bags of potatoes, carrots, onions and other fruits and vegetables. Many families here do not rely on processed, canned, or packaged food on Pesach, so the produce and eggs are in great demand. Shoppers were purchasing large quantities of these items. It was, so to speak, a spontaneous *shuk*. As I strode along I saw an impressive, well-kept fish tank with pretty goldfish swimming inside. This item attracted a group of children with an adult who were enjoying the scene. Next, I had the opportunity to say a rare *bracha*. When one sees fruit trees first blossom, one thanks *Hashem*. I saw a pear tree and an avocado tree displaying their first budding flowers, and next to the trees was a huge sign with the proper *bracha* written on it. So, I arrived at the dentist in good spirits!

I might add that this is the big season for companies who sell cleaning supplies; the newspapers are filled with ads for a plethora of effective cleaning products. By the way, children come home from nursery school with a paper dustpan to encourage them to help clean for Pesach. And, of course, the usual large metal vats with steaming hot water, manned by young boys, are available on our main street for residents to bring their pots and other utensils to *kasher* for Pesach. The local grocery store has covered all its counters and sealed off areas with *chametz*. People are hustling and bustling, creating a sense of energy and excitement in anticipation of the upcoming *chag*.

Motzaei Shabbat, April 30, 2011

Several days ago I returned from a spiritually inspiring, emotionally satisfying and physically refreshing Pesach visit to Kibbutz Chafetz Chayim. Shira and family joined me, enriching the experience immeasurably. Shlomo enlightened our meals with fascinating Torah commentary; Shira and I had a chance to play some recorder duets together; the older boys enjoyed cycling on the broad empty spaces, rarely available in B'nei Brak; my 10- and 12-year-old granddaughters made 14 friends; I was able to help my grandson Mordechai with his English reading; and my older grandson Menachem helped me to understand a lot of the Talmudic allusions in Shai Agnon's stories. As Shira said, the family prepared for Pesach for three months (they rented their apartment out for the holiday) and the wonderful memory of the eight days at the kibbutz will last for three years until it is their turn again to spend Pesach with me.

Upon my return to Yerushalayim, I'm reminded that during the midst of counting the Omer, we are anticipating the commemorative days of

Yom HaShoah, Yom HaZikaron, Yom HaAtzmaut, Lag BaOmer, and Yom Yerushalayim in the lead-up to the major festival, Shavuot. And politically, as I read in the papers, there is much concern here – maybe tension – regarding all the upheavals in our neighboring lands. Obviously, we're worried about how the instability of the governments will affect relations with us.

Shira and I are leaving imminently for our journey of several weeks to the States, where I look forward to seeing family and friends.

Monday, May 23, 2011

As Shira and I were departing for our journey to the U.S. on Yom HaShoah, we experienced a riveting few minutes. The departures terminal in Ben Gurion Airport – considered the nicest and most modern one in the Middle East – is huge. As the massive area was filled with people eagerly checking in for their impending flights, suddenly, at exactly 10:00 a.m., a long siren sounded. An eerie silence blanketed the giant premises as thousands of individuals stopped in their tracks for two minutes, standing silently, to pay homage to the victims of the Shoah. A very sobering experience.

This year I heard that on Lag BaOmer, the *yahrtzeit* of Rabbi Shimon Bar Yochai, more than three hundred thousand people made the trip to Mount Meron where they gathered to celebrate at the gravesite of this sage and scholar who lived in the immediate aftermath of the Second Temple. Unlike a regular *yahrtzeit*, which is marked with sadness and even fasting, the *yahrtzeit* of a great tzaddik is a *yom hillulah*, a day that is commemorated specifically through *simcha* and festive celebration. It was, as usual, well organized with free food, *medurot*, live music and dancing. Many people, particularly Chassidim, bring their three-year-old boys to Meron for their first haircut, known as *chalaka*, another tradition for Lag BaOmer in Meron. I heard on the radio that there was zero empty space. My grandson Simcha, with a group of his yeshiva friends, arrived at the mountain top on Friday afternoon and camped out celebrating Shabbat with several thousand other people. Simcha enjoyed the spectacular views from the mountain top. The major *medurah* was lit by the Boyaner Rebbe on Motzaei Shabbat and the crowds then intensified.

Several days before Lag BaOmer there were many alerts on the radio for the *medurot* throughout the country to be lit only in designated places and certainly not near any forests. I think most of the inhabitants of Bayit VeGan were at a major *medurah* in a large plaza nearby. The neighborhood was alive with the sound of music.

My newest word is *misrone* – meaning "text message" or "SMS" – and is related to the words *limsor* (to transmit), *meser* (message), and *masoret* (tradition).

Tuesday, June 7, 2011

Shira and I had a meaningful and emotional trip to the States connecting with many family members and friends. Since our trip included a stay in Philadelphia - where we visited the National Museum of American Jewish History, Congregation Mikveh Israel (the second oldest synagogue in the U.S.), Independence Hall, the Liberty Bell and other historical sites - I was able to regale my American friends in Israel with some memories of Philly. The primary purpose of my Philadelphia stay was to participate in the reunion of a group of Young Judaea Zionist youth leaders with whom I had made my first trip to Israel in 1955. I felt that just as I conveyed news of Lafayette and some historical Philadelphia spots to friends here, I was also able to be a *shlicha* (emissary) for Israel on my tour of the U.S.

Just after enjoying another exciting reunion recently in an upscale restaurant in Tel Aviv with my friends who had spent various lengths of time working at Purdue, I noticed that Purdue President France Anne Córdova was granted an honorary Ph.D. at Ben-Gurion University in Beer Sheva. She, along with University of Miami President Donna Shalala and two other women, university presidents in Israel, were saluted for breaking the glass ceiling.

Although the flower vendors on each block in my neighborhood do a brisk business every Friday, there are huge numbers of people buying flowers for the festive holiday of Shavuot when it is appropriate to decorate one's home with fresh blossoms and greenery.

Friday, June 17, 2011

One of my special moments last week was fulfilling the mitzvah of making people happy. This came about because my musical ensemble (we still haven't chosen a name) performed before a very responsive audience of elderly people at their social club. My ensemble now boasts seven musicians, including a singer who has an unusually wide singing range.

We are playing a combination of nostalgic music with an international theme. Some of our songs include those I arranged for the Lafayette Klezmorim. Maybe we'll be the Jerusalem Klezmorim? I don't know.

When one of my *ulpan* colleagues returned to class after being sick for quite a while, the teacher greeted her with *Baruch Rofeh Cholim* – Blessed is the Healer of the sick. I thought this was very touching.

FRIDAY, JULY 08, 2011

I recently learned that the Egged bus company offers a *cartis ma'avar* (transfer ticket), which, after paying the fare on your first bus, allows unlimited travel to any destination within greater Jerusalem, on as many buses as you can manage to board within an hour and twenty minutes. I hope this bargain will encourage some of my readers to visit Jerusalem!

I participate in four classes a week on Jewish subjects, two of which deal with Torah textual analysis and commentary; one is a lecture on the weekly Shabbat portion; and another discusses halachot and *minhagim*, as stated in the Gemara and *Shulchan Aruch*.

There's an expression "All roads lead to Rome." I was thinking that for a Jew, all roads lead to Jerusalem, and a parallel would be all days of the week lead up to Shabbat. One lecturer stressed the difference in the way non-Jews perceive the week, contrasting it with the Jewish view. He suggested that some people view their week by looking forward to the weekend for a break in the toil of the middle days of the week, while the Jewish view is to count each day in the following way: Sunday is *yom rishon*, literally, "the first day" until Shabbat, Monday is *yom sheini*, the second day until Shabbat, and so on with each day until the crowning event, Shabbat, which is the apex of the week. Shabbat preparations begin early in the week. In many *frum* neighborhoods, take-out food stores open Wednesday, Thursday and Friday with deliciously prepared victuals for Shabbat enjoyment. The progression gives us a golden opportunity to revel in our connection to *Hashem*.

I was saddened to learn of the death of Jonathan Pollard's father, Morris. *Baruch Dayan HaEmet*. He was a friend and colleague of Ed's. In the late '60s Ed was invited by Morris to speak in the biology department at Notre Dame. I came along, and we were invited to the Pollard home where we briefly met a teenaged Jonathan. Morris and his wife were our guests at Purdue, probably over 10 years ago, where Morris gave a talk about Jonathan's situation. We also visited with Morris shortly before Ed died.

On a happier note, I was invited with friends to an elegant tea party and fashion show. The fancy cakes were served on the veranda of a large building, with over 60 women seated around tables. We were serenaded by two musicians playing classical music. However, what was of special interest to me was to see a fashion show where the models were modestly attired. While they were tall, stately and beautiful, and the clothes were lovely and varied, all skirts were well below the knees, sleeves were below the elbows, necklines were high and there were neither pantsuits nor especially clingy materials! This show was geared to Orthodox women, most of whom probably were Chareidi.

Israel is famous for the number and quality of their *chevrot haznek* (startup companies). The word *lezanek* means "to leap or pounce." Interestingly, the term for driving a stick shift (manual transmission) uphill, after a stop, is *zinuk ba'aliya*.

And a useful expression I learned is *naylech al zeh*, meaning "Let's go for it." However, thanks to a friend I also learned the army slang *na'oof al zeh* – "Let's fly with it!"

Tuesday, July 19, 2011

Over the last few days I have noticed large black particles of dust that can't be easily swept away. It seems there was a major forest fire in the Jerusalem Forest, about three miles from my home, and this is the residue. I was told this fire was reported on the national media. It took me a little while to make the connection, since Jerusalem generally is very dusty during the long months without rain. The dust seems to seep in through unseen cracks and requires daily eliminating. This dust was different from the usual, for a sad reason.

My leadership abilities are being utilized as I am now in the midst of organizing several events. One was arranging a reunion of a few Israeli couples who had lived in Lafayette for a while. And of course I have my music ensemble, which now practices weekly and has a number of gigs in the offing. The big event, however, which I am now organizing, is the Israel Hoosier reunion. There are many families here – maybe 30 or more

– who are eager to come to my home after the *chaggim* to reunite with one another. Most families stem from Indianapolis and South Bend. And of course, planning my husband's fifth *yahrtzeit* is a major project, since I may have 30 family members from several continents attending. It occurs to me that the 12 years during which I was president of the Lafayette Chapter of Hadassah and the Sons of Abraham Sisterhood probably endowed me with or helped to hone these useful leadership skills.

Today is a fast day, the 17th of the Hebrew month of Tammuz, which commemorates the breaching of the walls of Jerusalem and starts the three-week mourning period - for the destruction of Jerusalem and our two Holy Temples - leading up to Tisha B'Av. My religious neighborhood is unusually quiet, traffic is at a minimum and many shops close early.

Tuesday, August 9, 2011

It is Tisha B'Av, and I have been able to fast the entire day with little distress. Part of my success, I think, is due to the fact that I stayed in my air-conditioned apartment and turned on the radio to hear *Eichah* (The Book of Lamentations) and various *kinot* (elegies recited to mourn the destruction of our two Holy Temples). Probably Israel is the only country where this is available. In past years I've had meaningful experiences listening to various rabbis giving English interpretations after chanting the *kinot*. These events take place in several locales. One year, my Yiddish teacher came to my home and read some *kinot* in Yiddish. Another annual traditional experience is walking on top of the walls of the Old City. Ed did that one year.

On this sad day, we sit on low stools and wear non-leather shoes. Since the fires in the Holy Temple were still burning on the following morning, we wait half a day before bathing, laundering, playing music, eating meat, drinking wine, and getting haircuts. May we have only happy occasions to celebrate in the future.

I now carry with me two additional cards. My identity card, which I've had since making aliyah, is a given. Not long ago, I acquired a Jerusalem Card, noting that I am a bona fide resident here and entitling me to discounts on various items including my hefty ulpan fee. Last week, I obtained my rechargeable Rav-Kav card, which will be used for the new digital system that should soon, I think, be installed on buses as well as on the new light rail. *Rav-Kav* means "many transportation lines."

Since I generally travel by taxi and was advised not to ride the train for a few weeks after it accepts passengers, I imagine I'll use my newest card rarely.

Motzaei Shabbat, August 20, 2011

Last week we celebrated Shabbat Nachamu to comfort us after our mourning on Tisha B'Av and to help raise our mood to enjoy Tu B'Av, one of the happiest days on the Jewish calendar. Just as Valentine's Day is the busiest time of the year for flower dealers in the U.S., Tu B'Av is the Israeli equivalent. Sometimes referred to as the Jewish Valentine's day, Tu B'Av comes six days after Tisha B'Av and celebrates the occasion when young men in ancient days could choose brides from amongst girls who went out "dressed in white and danced in the vineyards" [Tractate *Taanit*, Chapter 4]. Today, it is a day when many people choose to marry, since it comes shortly after the period of time when traditionally no Jewish weddings are performed.

Since all schools are on vacation now, Israelis are on wheels. As we have four climatic zones in our small country, it is possible to vacation in different climates and topographies with relative ease.

To spoil this idyllic time, we suffered a tragic *pigua* (terrorist attack) close to the southern city of Eilat, which is near the Egyptian border. For two days, Israelis were glued to their radios to learn what was happening and to listen to the names of the dead being buried. I discussed this sad news with my cab driver, a tough-looking man, no yarmulke, probably Sephardic. His response to the events was, "Everyone needs to do *teshuvah*," meaning we need to become more observant, do more mitzvot, and examine our relationship with *Hashem* so He will protect us and give us the strength to defend ourselves. As I alighted from the cab I said, "We should only hear *besorot tovot*" (good tidings). His reply was, "For all the nation of Israel." Tragically, the terror continues.

Israel is a living, energetic, vibrant society. It's also a country with striking contrasts. If you take Chareidim and *chilonim*, Sephardim and Ashkenazim, young and old, poor and rich, Arabs and Jews, you have all these differences. They make Israeli society so *leibedig* (joyful). And because we are so dynamic and spirited, this mosaic of a society, we are able to develop so many innovations. We are creating energy. That's the Jewish people's history, and that's the State of Israel. It's this creative energy that people do not understand, because when somebody comes and writes about Israel, he's focusing on the state of conflict, and that's not the main point.

Yesterday, the Jerusalem Light Rail accepted passengers for its maiden public voyage. Rides will be free for the first few weeks, due to problems with the ticketing system. Also, since appropriate traffic lights have not yet been installed, the journey – from Mount Herzl in southwest Jerusalem, passing through East Jerusalem, and ending up in the northern part of the city, in Pisgat Ze'ev – will be 70 minutes instead of the projected 40 minutes. Apparently, there were dozens of policemen and hundreds of ushers along the tracks, answering questions and directing passengers. It's a big day for Jerusalem residents!

Shira and five of her children spent almost a week with me. Shlomo loves to come here from B'nei Brak for the mountain air. The family took in various sights including the very interesting Menchem Begin Heritage Center. They were impressed with the experience. We recollected a quote from Begin when he was handed a letter by former President Carter, in 1978, asking him to sign on the subject of negotiating the status of Jerusalem. He refused to sign, saying, "For 2,000 years, we Jews have been reciting a verse from King David's Psalms at every wedding ceremony: 'If I forget thee, O Jerusalem, may my right hand lose her cunning; let my tongue cleave to the roof of my mouth, if I hold thee not above my highest joy.'"

Carter then asked, "But doesn't your Jewish law maintain that you must give up a limb in order to save the entire organism?" "Yes," said Begin, "but not if the limb is one's heart. Jerusalem is the heart of Israel, the heart of the Jewish people. It is our heart and it is non-negotiable."

I was pleased to host my 16-year-old grandson from Milwaukee for two and a half weeks following a very positive experience in Israel with his National Council of Synagogue Youth camp. NCSY brought 2,000 teenagers, ages 14-18, to Israel this summer. During his stay with me, Yechiel went frequently to his friend in B'nei Brak with whom he learns Jewish subjects. The rest of the time, his cousins invited him and me for some quality family time and delicious meals. Yechiel also did some sightseeing, such as visiting the Herzl Museum nearby as well as Mini Israel—a park featuring miniature models of Israel's most important historical, religious, archeological and modern sites, located in Latrun, halfway between Jerusalem and Tel Aviv. He visited his cousins' yeshivot and enjoyed touring Geula, the section of

Jerusalem where religious kids shop and "hang out" on Friday afternoons. Upon his departure, Yechiel said, "This was the best summer in my whole life."

Coke, which is called Cola here, just put on the market a cardboard box that holds six bottles with special Shabbat labeling, featuring two challot, two Shabbat candles and a *Kiddush* cup. The packaging obviates the need to tear letters, which is prohibited when opening on Shabbat. The legend says "Coca-Cola is happy to be part of your *Oneg Shabbat* each week anew. Shabbat Shalom!" There is a game board on the inside of the carton that is appropriate for Shabbat, with the bottle caps becoming the game pieces.

My granddaughter Yocheved and her husband, Yehoshua, who live here, enjoyed an amazing two-hour hike in the Jerusalem hills. Their well-signed trail featured fulsome foliage and stunning scenery. They came upon a freshwater natural spring, which created a swimming hole that was enjoyed by some children. Yocheved and Yehoshua chose not to immerse.

I never cease to enjoy unexpected encounters. When Yocheved and Yehoshua completed their recent little hike in the hills of Jerusalem, they found themselves far from the possibility of any public transportation and were concerned as to how they would manage to get home. By chance, they came upon a friendly family who offered them a lift to a bus stop when the pater familias would come by in his large jeep. When the transport arrived, the driver was an Englishman from London. Within a very few minutes it transpired that Yehoshua was the first cousin of the father's son-in-law and had been at his wedding. This unexpectedly close relationship coupled with the driver's kindness merited the hikers a lift directly to their home.

Thursday, August 25, 2011

In my last missive I described a beguiling hike through the Jerusalem hills taken by my grandchildren. Shortly after penning that e-mail, a friend visited and related to me that he takes a similar trek, daily, in the early morning. He described some interesting details of the area. Sataf was one of the many nearby Arab villages to be deserted in the 1948 Israeli War of Independence. There are two freshwater springs in the remains of the village. One creates a pond. The second spring, called Ein Sataf, emanates from a deep mountain cavern and creates the freshwater swimming hole, which Yocheved and Yehoshua saw. My friend said that fresh goat cheese is readily available from a nearby goatherd and also commented that there are ancient terraces, constructed thousands of years ago by our ancestors. Today, families are granted individual plots of several meters on these timeless terraces on which they plant their own vegetable gardens. He continued to describe a rare phenomenon. As you know, the summer here is sunny, long and dry, but sometimes the sky is partly cloudy. The eucalyptus trees, with their broad, thick branches, under which the hikers walk, convert the moisture in these clouds to a light rain. Immediately upon passing through the eucalyptus grove, the rain ceases.

I offer these tantalizing details in the hope that some of my readers will consider enjoying an amazing hike through the ancient, holy hills of Jerusalem.

Wednesday, September 21, 2011

Each of my taxi drivers in the past several days has wished me *Shanah Tovah*. People are shopping frenetically and the airport predicts well over a million travelers in the next few days. Tomorrow, my 12-year-old granddaughter and I expect to be two of them, traveling to Milwaukee for the bat mitzvah of my granddaughter Rivka. Our stay in the Midwest is planned to include a brief visit to physicians and friends in Lafayette.

One reason the produce here is so tasty is that it doesn't have to be flown in from elsewhere. Yocheved commented that, for example, in the winter when our bodies need vitamin C, citrus fruits and the abundant pomegranates are plentifully available; and in the summer when we must drink a great deal, the often small, sweet and seedless watermelons can quench our thirst.

Some new words I've learned are: *moofin* – muffin (cupcakes and muffins are not so popular here); *oomtza*, a modern word meaning "steak," borrowed from the Aramaic of the Babylonian Talmud; *nogdan* – antibody; *mirkam* – texture; *pancher* or *neker* – a flat tire; *pancheria* – a tire repair service; and *kaldanut* – word processing, or computer typing.

Several weeks ago, a friend commented that there is a hunger for Jewish tradition among the *chiloni* segment of the population. I recently noticed a few articles in *The Jerusalem Post* corroborating his remarks. The first headline is "Megila Readings Find Widening Appeal among the Secular Public." Another reads, "Religious Pluralism on Shavuot: No longer the exclusive domain of the Orthodox, Shavuot night has become a nightlong learn-in for the religious and secular." I must say that through the years in Lafayette, Ed and I sponsored many learn-ins on Shavuot night, when we had various people give short talks on a variety of Jewish subjects, accompanied by tasty dairy delights.

I found some information of interest about Jerusalem, which I'll add to my previous thoughts:

> *Jerusalem has been blessed with extraordinary cultural diversity.... expressed in the city's educational institutions....Jerusalem boasts a host of unique and unusual schools of every kind and creed — state, state-religious, Ultra-Orthodox and Arab....The diverse communities, beliefs, practices and preferences of Jerusalem's residents and educational institutions, in addition to the sheer size of Jerusalem's educational system, have proven a rather fertile ground for educational innovation of the highest order. As such, it has become a paradigm of excellence in the field of education and a model to be emulated throughout the rest of the country...*
> [*The Jerusalem Post,* April 5, 2011]

Another item of interest:

> *Massachusetts is home to nearly 100 companies with Israeli founders or Israeli-licensed technologies....Massachusetts "came to the decision that Israel is a country with which it wants to work, with which it wants to trade and cooperate," [economist Hadas] Bar-Or said....the Israel-US Binational Industrial Research and Development Foundation...approved a major initiative last week: an $8.1 million investment in nine new bilateral projects, including advanced developments in life sciences and information technology for medical applications.*
> [*The Jerusalem Post,* July 7, 2011]

And a headline from five weeks ago:

Israel's hi-tech workforce climbs to 198,500
Hi-tech employees make up 8.4% of the business sector, responsible for 16% of business product.
[*The Jerusalem Post,* August 12, 2011]

One of the most popular satirists of the world, the late Ephraim Kishon, penned numerous pithy remarks during his illustrious career. Although most of these were written perhaps 40 years ago, my son Rashi thought that they bear repeating, so I include a few in this letter:

- Israel is one of the few places in the world where the sun sets into the Mediterranean Sea.
- Israel is the only country in the world where the graffiti is in Hebrew.
- Israel is the only country in the world with bus drivers and taxi drivers who read [and quote] Spinoza and Maimonides.
- Israel is the only country in the world where inviting someone "out for a drink" means drinking cola, coffee or tea.
- Israel is the only country in the world where "small talk" consists of loud, angry debate over politics and religion.

I wish my family and friends a *Ketivah Va-Chatimah Tovah* and a healthy, sweet year.

Motzaei Shabbat, October 15, 2011

I was very happy to see many friends during my brief visit to Lafayette. I appreciate everyone who made the effort to welcome me, my daughter Ronit, and my granddaughter Chana from Israel. I was somewhat sad taking leave of so many families whom I had known well for numerous years. In many cases, I had taught their children and remember them vividly. There were several people I missed and hope to catch up with on another occasion. In Milwaukee, I was happy to participate in the beautiful bat mitzvah celebration of my granddaughter Rivka Tzipora Sara. *Mazal Tov* to her parents and siblings.

Whenever I travel by taxi, I try to bring 20- or 50-shekel notes to have when paying the driver, and I always insist on the *moneh* (meter). Some people do well at bargaining; not I. Usually I say out loud what change is due me, but less than half a shekel is generally forgotten. I have learned to recognize which drivers are Arabs, and the vast majority of my taxi trips are very pleasant. I make the trip to my *ulpan* regularly, so I am able to direct the driver to my preferred route. I've learned that the younger drivers generally seem to be more alert in picking up a signal from a potential passenger standing on the edge of the sidewalk, and they will often give me a more rapid ride. Most drivers are quiet, which I really prefer since I often read or sometimes rest during my journeys. A few steps from my building I only need to wait from about five seconds to four minutes for a taxi. So far, traveling by taxi is a buyer's market. My son Rashi suggests I write a chapter about my taxi experiences.

The electrifying news recently is that Gilad Shalit, who was kidnapped over five years ago by Hamas, should soon be returning home! My great-niece Dalia, who is studying in seminary this year, went to the Shalit tent to dance with the throngs of young people who are celebrating. The radio continues to give the names, the crimes and the destinations of the 15 most wanted terrorists who are among the over 1,000 to be exchanged. There are many bereaved families who are upset by the release of these terrorists with blood on their hands, and all hope Israel is prepared to protect its citizens should there be renewed attacks. I heard that before they can be released, the terrorists have to sign a document that they won't resort again to terrorism.

My musical ensemble, now named Manginot Me-HaOlam (Melodies from around the World), has just entertained at several senior citizens' residences and received very warm receptions. I'm the director, conductor, alto recorder player and shtick master, though I can never be as effective as the shtick master from my Lafayette Klezmorim ensemble. Our pianist is a talented composer and lyricist, and we showcase one or two of her songs at each performance. Our violinist has the gift of easily harmonizing. Our singer has a clear, true and high soprano voice as well as a rich background in Yiddish songs. We are a group of seven mainly mature women and we are having fun.

On Ed's 5th *yahrtzeit*, Chol HaMo'ed Sukkot, I am planning a seminar here focusing on Ed's relationship with his children. I already have next year's subject planned: his relationship with his grandchildren and graduate students. This year over 30 family members, including a large contingent from abroad, plan to participate. We shall say *tehillim* at Ed's graveside and then adjourn to a restaurant where we will conclude the evening with a joyous celebration of my granddaughter Zeesy's bat mitzvah.

The following night I expect about 75 former Hoosiers to reunite at my home. We are creating an Indiana *landsmannschaft*. I plan to write a report after the reunion.

There is a new exhibition at the Bible Lands Museum displaying shofrot and examining their resounding role in Jewish history. *The Jerusalem Post's* description says: "From a shofar used in the 17th century to proclaim excommunication to one made in a Romanian labor camp during the Holocaust, the instrument has accompanied Jews from their darkest periods to their greatest joys."

Some seasoned Lafayette shul members may recall that Ed was the shofar blower for the High Holidays for about 20 years. I recall his traipsing up and down Rechov Allenby, a major Tel Aviv thoroughfare, testing various shofrot so that he could choose the one that suited him best. This year, after Yom Kippur, one of my many musically talented grandchildren, Yehuda Aharon, blew Ed's shofar in London, at his father's shul.

Rebbitzen Batsheva Kanievsky died very suddenly at her home in B'nei Brak this Shabbat afternoon. One is not allowed to mourn on Shabbat, so her husband continued learning until nightfall when he then burst into tears. Rabbi Chaim Kanievsky is a well-known tzaddik and *gaon* (brilliant Talmudic scholar), and his rebbitzen was known as a major *tzaddeket*. Countless men and women from across the religious spectrum stood in line to seek her warmth and counsel and receive *brachot* from her. She had impeccable integrity and was an admired role model. She will be buried tonight, directly after Shabbat, with probably tens of thousands of mourners - including Shira and Shlomo - following her coffin. Sadly, her esteemed aged father, Rabbi Yosef Shalom Elyashiv, who is still very alert, has lost several of his children. However, interestingly, he was an only child and has lived to see over a thousand descendants. May the rebbitzen's memory be for a blessing.

Israel is justly proud of its recent Nobel Prize winner from Haifa, Professor Dan Shechtman. I read an interesting anecdote. The South Korean ambassador to Israel visited several yeshivot in B'nei Brak in an effort to find the secret of the Jews, who while being only 0.2 percent of the world population have won 22 percent of the Nobel Prizes. He thought the secret formula was the constant study of the Talmud. It occurred to the ambassador that if the South Koreans would study like the Jews, they would win more Nobels. So, his wife gifted him with a complete set of the Talmud for his birthday.

Most shuls auction off their High Holiday *aliyot la-Torah* for money, deeming those special opportunities worthy of great honor. The monies garnered also bring in necessary funds for the shul. Recently, my grandson Simcha informed me that the currency for the auction in his Israeli yeshiva is not money but a commitment to learn a specific amount of Gemara in the coming year. As I understand, the person who wins the *aliyah* must fulfill the pledge or pay a shekel per folio page. I believe this commitment is on the honor system. Simcha bought a major *aliyah* at great "expense," and he assures me he is keeping up with his obligation, in addition to his regular yeshiva studies.

Motzaei Shabbat, November 12, 2011

This week was the *yahrtzeit* of Rachel Imeinu and many thousands of people took the opportunity to go to her *kever* and daven. They poured out their hearts, as the image is "Mameh Rochel" crying for her children. This gives them comfort and hope. Her grave, which now has a large structure built around it, is about half a kilometer (a quarter of a mile) south of Jerusalem, on the outskirts of the city of Bethlehem, along the way to Chevron where our forefathers are buried. Many people mark the occasion with *yahrtzeit* candles and special commemorations in their homes.

Very sadly, on the same day, the prominent *rosh yeshiva* of Mir, Rabbi Nosson Tzvi Finkel, died. All the yeshivot and seminaries canceled their studies and the students were bused to the cemetery where well over 100,000 people gathered for the funeral. Before and after, there were moving and impressive eulogies. Born in Chicago, Rabbi Finkel came to Israel and built up the Mir Yeshiva – with a large campus and many buildings – into one of the most prominent scholarly institutions in the world. He was known, from his youth on, as an exceptionally diligent person and as someone who dedicated himself to learning and inspired thousands of others to do likewise. He was a role model for overcoming obstacles in order to achieve scholarly goals. Despite suffering from Parkinson's in his later years, he traveled the world over to raise money for the yeshiva's 6,000 students and when in Jerusalem continued his daily lectures to them. *Baruch Dayan HaEmet*.

A week ago Thursday evening was the date when we add the words *v'ten tal umatar livracha* in our daily prayers for the duration of the winter. Although on Shmini Atzeret we recite a long, special prayer for rain, we remember the travelers of ancient days who needed to return to their distant homes in Israel after making a pilgrimage to Jerusalem. Out of consideration for their lengthy journey, this short prayer for dew and rain is inserted two weeks later. In the rest of the world, which follows a solar rather than our lunar calendar, the date for including that prayer is December 4th (or December 5th, in every secular year preceding a secular leap year). It actually did rain the day we starting praying for it, and my grandson-in-law told of seeing a five-year-old boy dancing happily down the street with his hands upturned to the raindrops and singing *gishmei bracha* (rain that brings blessing).

Adjacent to Jerusalem is a lovely new city called Beitar. I had wanted to see it since it is relatively close by and a number of my friends have children living there. My chance came when my grandson Saadia, who was visiting from Baltimore, had an appointment with his teacher at his former yeshiva in Beitar. He kindly took me along. Beitar is a pretty, new city with modern structures, attractive lampposts and good transportation to Jerusalem. At the yeshiva, since women generally don't enter the *beit midrash* (study hall), I had an opportunity to look down on close to 75 young men sitting, either facing one another, or adjacent to one another, each with his Gemara on his *shtender* (book stand), gesticulating and talking to one another with electric energy. Although I had seen pictures of this phenomenon, it was exciting for me to observe the action to my heart's content, from a floor above.

Three of my grandsons enjoyed an unusually beautiful desert hike near an oasis called Ein Mabua. A large array of multicolored wildflowers presented a breathtaking sight. The lilac-like foliage emitting a beguiling aroma and the clear spring water that formed a freshwater swimming pool made the experience memorable. What is exceptional is that this oasis is on the road to Jericho, which is Israeli/Jordanian territory and can only be reached by taxi or private car. The area was protected by a host of Israeli rangers.

Several days after Simchat Torah, over 55 former Hoosiers gathered in my home for a reunion. The warmth, the emotion, the positive vibes, and the welcoming atmosphere created a very successful evening. Some comments afterward were: "The most fun we had in ages"; "I spoke to so many people that there was no time for any in-depth conversation"; "The warm pleasant surroundings, the joy of seeing so many former friends, the happy emotion that prevailed made us eager to plan for next year's get together." As my daughter-in-law Ruthie said, "There was a lot of buzz in that room."

How did this all begin? About six months ago, I met a woman in my *ulpan* whose husband had been the founding principal of Hasten Hebrew Academy in Indianapolis. She still kept in close touch with many members of the committee who helped establish the school in the early '70s. I suggested that we make plans for a Hoosier-Israeli reunion. By each of us contacting several people we knew, and with essential help from two friends, we were able to create a database of 74 names. We did include several families who have children here and visit at frequent intervals. Former Hoosiers came from Alon Shvut, Beer Sheva, Kfar Chabad, Beit Shemesh, Jerusalem and other locales. We had people who were new immigrants, here only several months, as well as others who have been in Israel as long as 40 years.

The timing was planned, at first, to accommodate my children. I don't want them to forget their Indiana roots, and I knew they expected to be in Israel for Ed's *yahrtzeit*, which we commemorated the day before the reunion. However, very fortuitously, a number of prominent Indy families were visiting here at the same time. My co-chair, Judy Epstein, prepared name tags and checked e-mail addresses as people entered. Shira welcomed guests outside the building, Ronit stayed by the door greeting attendees as they entered and departed, Rashi gave some welcoming remarks during the evening, and Hillel took pictures. I made a tape of background music: the Indiana state song, "On the Banks of the Wabash," and "Back Home Again in Indiana." Rabbi Gray gave some very delightful and welcome remarks, and a really good time was had by all.

Thanksgiving is approaching and my friend asked me if Chareidi Americans here celebrate the occasion. After a very brief survey I concluded that they do not. However, there are quite a few non-Chareidi American expats who do celebrate Thanksgiving here. I've even heard of some who prepare their Shabbat meal with the holiday trimmings. The Orthodox schools with which I'm familiar in the States have classes half a day for religious studies only; since it's a legal holiday, there are no secular classes. Anyhow, here I have been almost completely unaware of Thanksgiving, with the exception of one friend, non-religious, who does mark the day with her family.

Tuesday, November 29, 2011

Several days ago I sat outside the entryway of my apartment building at 2:45 p.m. on a gray day and watched a crowd of at least 500 people gather rather promptly for a funeral, blocking the entire corner of my busy street to vehicular traffic. As is common in my neighborhood, men stood in one area and women opposite them. A large loudspeaker was put into place, soon to be used to amplify the eulogies given by about five people. The immense group stood silently and respectfully. From 11:30 a.m., large notices were pasted on the outside of my building, and in the early afternoon, a car with a large megaphone broadcast throughout the streets the death of my beloved neighbor Devora Suissa. Cars with loudspeakers announcing the death of someone in the neighborhood is the typical way of communicating the news in Chareidi areas.

After about an hour, over 300 people accompanied the hearse by foot along one of the main streets in Bayit VeGan. Of course, vehicular traffic had to accommodate the mourners. Eventually they would board buses to take them to the cemetery.

Friday, December 2, 2011

This has been a sad week. The 14 adult Suissa children sat shivah with their father in their parents' home, one floor above my apartment, so I was able to see some of the thousands of visitors who came to console the family. Of course, the 12 spouses and the older grandchildren were there to provide for the needs of the mourners.

My neighbor Devora was born in a villa (single home), which stood on the same spot that my apartment house now occupies. Her father, a well-to-do businessman, came to Israel from Poland in the 1930s. He married here and had several daughters. Although he worked in Tel Aviv, he so loved Jerusalem. The story goes that the city wanted to build a sports stadium in a nearby vacant area, and since Bayit VeGan is a neighborhood designated for schools and yeshivot, Devora's father, Mr. Araten, lobbied the government to designate the land for reasonably priced apartments for *avreichim* (young married men learning full-time in kollel). A compromise was reached and the city created a lovely park with trees, grass, comfortable benches, and play equipment for children. Mr. Araten was in the plant and nursery business and donated all of the trees in the park, which now bears his name. He himself planted an especially big sapling, which still stands in his memory.

Unfortunately, Mr. Araten was widowed and just after the war married a young dentist recently arrived from Berlin. In 1947 their only child, Devora, was born. Devora remembered the dental clinic that occupied part of their home during her childhood and the many needy patients her mother treated, often at no charge. Next to their house was an orphanage, which Devora's father supported. He noticed a very capable teacher there, originally from Morocco, and thought that this man would be a good match for his daughter. The couple married and proceeded to raise an outstanding family together.

Devora's work outside the home was as a *balanit*. She did her work so capably that she was soon asked to teach other women to be "*mikveh* ladies." By periodically traveling to various ritual baths in the city, Devora would make sure the *balaniyot* were well prepared and the standards were kept high.

By the time I moved into my apartment, Devora had retired from her *mikveh* work. What made me love and admire her were her amazing *midot* (character traits). She was generous to a fault, remembering my birthday with a small present, giving me gifts for the various holidays, and tendering a standing invitation to join her family on Shabbat. It is a Jewish *minhag* to accompany visitors to the door and even four *amot* (6-8 feet) further. Like our forefather Abraham who accompanied his guests a short distance upon their departure, Devora, after every visit of mine, was particular in fulfilling this mitzvah. Even when she could no longer walk, she would wheel her wheelchair into the hallway to watch me descend the stairs to my apartment.

One of Devora's three American daughters-in-law told me that although she appreciated her own parents' relationship with her husband and her brother's spouse, there was no doubt that Devora was an outstanding mother-in-law, adored and admired by all the spouses of her children. I'm impressed by the respect and harmony I've seen in the home—no small feat for a couple blessed with such a large family. When I was at her Shabbat table, despite the many children and guests, she made a point of personally serving her husband. It's also interesting to see that the *b'chor* (firstborn son) takes foremost responsibility for helping the parents. It seems biblical to me to realize how much leadership is vested in the *b'chor*.

Before she died, Devora called each of her 14 children individually to give them a blessing and some personal advice, as did our forefather Yaakov when he blessed each of his sons. She included in her will that there should be no arguments over money, the children should all be good to one another and that they should respect the leadership of the *b'chor*. Finally, as this *tzaddeket* expired at home, at the age of 64, all 14 of her children were at her bedside at the moment she drew her last breath. I will miss her.

Sunday, December 18, 2011

I read that the measure of a society is shown by the frequency of random acts of kindness. I have experienced a number of these courtesies. For example, when I am carrying a heavy bag of garbage to the neighborhood bin, a passer-by will frequently offer to help me carry the bag and toss it into the container. Also, when I sometimes have difficulty exiting from a taxi, a woman nearby will extend a hand and help me out. My grandson Simcha was foraging in his pockets for his bus fare, to no avail. A nearby passenger paid his fare for him. "That would never have happened in England," Simcha reported. A friend was shopping at a take-out food store while holding a young baby in one arm, and a cashier offered to hold the infant while he shopped. He appreciated this unusually thoughtful *chesed*.

While I go to Tel Aviv rarely, last week I enjoyed the opera in the awesome opera house. I saw *Cavalleria Rusticana* and *Pagliacci*. My father had taken me to these operas in New York when I was a youngster, and I still remembered some of the well-known arias from each production. I was enthralled with the whole experience. The next day I lunched at a restaurant in the Azrieli Towers with some Israelis who had spent several years in Lafayette. At the entrance to the towers there were five large statues of klezmer musicians, each playing an instrument. That was the first time I had ever seen a group of statues of klezmorim.

I read some background about Tel Aviv's historical buildings. Although the city was founded in 1909 making it much younger than the major European and American urban centers, the city fathers decided to preserve about 400 historical buildings, many of which were in the Bauhaus style. I learned that Tel Aviv is the Bauhaus capital of the world and in 2003 UNESCO declared it a World Heritage Site. The Bauhaus architectural style flourished in Germany in the 1930s. It has clean, functional lines and aesthetic beauty. Jewish refugees who had fled Nazi Germany built many such buildings in Tel Aviv. In World War II the British Royal Air Force and the U.S. Air Force bombarded German cities and as a result, most of the world's remaining Bauhaus buildings are found in Tel Aviv. Some experts believe that the Bauhaus style's popularity in this part of the world is due to its adaptation to our climate. The original architects created cool, spacious and comfortable dwellings. The Bauhaus style might have been the initiator of the rooftop garden, since they were the first buildings in Tel Aviv with strong flat roofs that were ideal for the creation of such gardens.

My musical ensemble has been practicing regularly. Last week our group performed for a local women's organization, similar to Hadassah. I was particularly proud of our program, which featured a good variety of familiar and new tunes, as well as diversified numbers. True to our name, Manginot Me-HaOlam, we played a Russian Sher; "Turkey in the Straw" with exceptionally witty words; and six hands on one piano (a piano trio) of "Stars and Stripes Forever"—the latter two representing America. We included some Italian waltzes, such as "O Sole Mio," and since many in the audience were from Great Britain, we played the medieval "Greensleeves" and the Irish song "Londonderry Air" ("Danny Boy"). Our presentation included two original pieces by our very talented pianist and composer, as well as a host of Chanukah songs. I was especially pleased to introduce a lyrical Italian-Sephardic melody to the familiar words of "Maoz Tzur"; a Yiddish song from my childhood called "Oy Ir Kleine Lichtelach" ("O You Small Candles"); and the familiar "Oy Chanukah," which we sang in Yiddish and Hebrew, known to most Americans as "Oh Chanukah, Oh Chanukah, Come Light the Menorah." Finally, we played a delightful, catchy Portuguese Ladino tune, "Una Kandelika." Our encore was "Sisu Et Yerushalayim" ("Rejoice with Jerusalem").

I wish all my friends and family a light-filled and festive Chanukah!

Chapter 5

2012

Sunday, January 22, 2012

This weekend I hosted friends from Chicago who were visiting their daughter currently learning in Michlala, a nearby seminary. Several of their daughter's friends also joined us for Shabbat and provided lively conversation, erudite *divrei Torah* and much good humor. With teamwork, including ordering some food, cooking some here, and lots of help in serving and clearing up, the 12 people around the table enjoyed a redemptive Shabbat *ruach*.

Recently in the news, there were reports of some unpleasant encounters instigated by an extremist group of Chareidim in Beit Shemesh. I attend a number of classes given by Chareidi rabbis, who each deviated briefly from his prepared lecture to strongly castigate the perpetrators of the tension between various religious communities, clearly distancing the mainstream majority of Chareidim from the lawless activities of one tiny Chassidic group.

Several weeks ago the *Indiana Jewish Post and Opinion* printed a large article with pictures of the huge and very successful Hoosiers-in-Israel reunion, which a friend and I hosted in my home. We received so many positive comments that I hope the reunion will become a yearly event.

I read in *The Jerusalem Post* some statistics about the minority community of Christians in Jerusalem. The article stated that by the end of 2010 this group constituted 1.9 percent of the capital's total population, or 14,600. Jerusalem is the only city in the world that has some 15 different Christian communities. Church clergy, monks, nuns and representatives of various Christian organizations reside here, and most churches and denominations seek to establish a presence here. Christian tourism is an important source of income for the country. Approximately 66 percent of the tourists who visited Israel and Jerusalem in 2010 were Christians, compared to 30 percent Jews.

My sister-in-law Harriet and her family spent an active week here, mainly to enjoy time with Harriet's granddaughter who is attending seminary in Jerusalem this year. Included among the various sites they visited are: the Silence Exhibition in Holon's Children's Museum, a three-hour tour through Jerusalem's City of David, and a hike on a hidden trail in the vicinity of the nearby Jerusalem Forest. They also hiked in the north, near Haifa, commencing in a valley near Mount Carmel and continuing for two hours up the mountain range, delighting in the views of Haifa University and the Technion (Israel Institute of Technology). The guide pointed out a flower, a type of pure white rose that grows nowhere else in the world and only blossoms several times a year on the Carmel range.

Harriet's son, Glen, hosted several family dinners in different restaurants. That seemed a gracious and efficient way to see a lot of people, given his limited stay here. I find that generally the food in restaurants is very fresh, portions are generous (I usually bring home some part of the meal to serve as my next day's lunch) and prices are reasonable. The milchig restaurants greatly outnumber the fleishig.

Recently, my grandson Dovid, who is learning here in yeshiva this year, was invited for Shabbat to Modi'in. He commented on the newness of the buildings and on their pretty blue rooftops. There is a great deal of construction there, as it is conveniently located about half way between Jerusalem and Tel Aviv. Modi'in is a fast-growing community comprising mainly a Modern Orthodox population.

More of Kishon:
- Israel is the only country in the world where everyone strikes up conversations while waiting in lines. [Except they don't wait in lines!]
- Israel is the only country in the world where people call an

attaché case a "James Bond" and the "@" sign is called a "strudel."
- Israel is the only country in the world where no one has a foreign accent because everyone has a foreign accent.
- Israel is the only country in the world where there is the most mysterious and mystical calm ambience in the streets on Yom Kippur, which cannot be explained unless you have experienced it.

Everyone here is happy when there is rain, but people are especially happy when there is snow on the Golan Heights. My taxi driver said, "That snow will melt into the Kinneret, and it will help lift the curse of the constant water shortage in this country."

Motzaei Shabbat, February 18, 2012

Shopping at the Machaneh Yehudah market can be a learning experience for someone unused to it. My grandson Dovid from London was told that an inexpensive place to buy pajamas would be the well-known Jerusalem market. He related two startling encounters. He entered a stall asking the price of shoes and the storekeeper, rather than responding, lured him in and insisted that he try on various pairs of shoes. He knew he didn't have the money to buy shoes and after revealing that he just wanted an estimate, the owner summarily took him by the collar and booted him out. He also learned that it is helpful to have an amount of small change, because the vendors want to sell the produce quickly, especially on Erev Shabbat, and you can often offer a few shekalim less than the suggested amount and the vendor will accept it. Dovid was even offered a discount because he is learning in a yeshiva. At my *ulpan*, I learned that veteran Jerusalemites would not let a week pass without their visit to the *shuk*, despite sales in supermarkets or nearby produce shops. Shopping Friday morning at the Machaneh Yehudah market is a crowded, colorful, aromatic and boisterous experience.

Accompanied by my teenage granddaughter Fraidy, Dovid's sister who is learning in seminary here this year, I had my first experience riding the Jerusalem Light Rail. We went to a framer in central Jerusalem who, much to my delight, framed my large picture in 20 minutes while we waited, and we decided to return by the light rail. The last stop is about a 12-minute walk from my home. I depended on Fraidy to help me with the embarking procedures. There are automated machines at each station in which one can insert a Rav-Kav card and pay for a series of trips, getting a receipt in return. This card can then be used for bus fare also. Upon entering the train there is a machine that accepts your card and lights up to let you know the number of rides remaining. An advantage for me is that there are no steps to enter or disembark. And although I had to stand, it was easy to hold onto the handbar and the ride was so smooth I wasn't jostled at all. Problems such as pedestrian safety and malfunctioning machines still need to be worked out, but my first experience was not unpleasant.

Israelis are absolutely enthralled with snow, at least those living in the center and south of the country. Many have never seen snow, and the merest mention of the possibility of a few flakes becomes the subject of animated conversation. My Israeli grandson recently said to me, excitedly, "Bubby, did you know that snow is predicted?" In a quick flashback, I reviewed the early snowy mornings in Indiana when I needed to clean the snow and ice off of the windshield, bundle the kids into the car, drive down an incline to pick up the other child carpooling with us – feeling fearful that the car wouldn't make it up the hill – and convey everyone to school. So I blurted out to my grandson, "I hate snow!" Stunned, he shook his head ruefully, and remarked, "Bubby, you are not an Israeli." However, a practical benefit of snow on the Golan Heights is that as it melts it descends into the Kinneret thus helping to raise the water level. Jerusalem has indeed had a few snowflakes. My neighbor's eight-year-old son collected several transient flakes and brought them in for us to see before they melted. Having come from much harsher climates in the U.S., I am still amazed at people's attitudes and unpreparedness for snow.

We are now in the midst of several continuous days of stormy winds and constant rain. My friend, who has lived here over 40 years, says she has never seen so many heavy winds and rain lasting for four or five days. Because we have been blessed with bountiful rains this winter, I hear people talking about the fact that the water level in the Kinneret has risen a few centimeters above the lower red line and is climbing to optimum level – with three and a half more meters to go.

I read an article entitled "Rediscovery of the Koseves": "For the first time in 2,000 years, the world's largest variety of date, referred to in the Talmud as *koseves gasa*, has been grown in Eretz Yisrael." As I understand, this huge rare date, with a volume larger than an egg, was referred to frequently in the Mishnah pertaining to various laws. The article tells how "the life span of the date palm is relatively short – fewer than 100 years. The only way a tree can naturally transfer its DNA to the next generation is by having new saplings taken from it planted every 10 years. Naturally, this necessitates continuous settlement, without wars or other signs of instability. The end of Jewish life in the Land of Israel after the destruction of the second Holy Temple also signaled the end of agricultural life."

Israeli botanists learned that *koseves* dates were being grown in Saudi Arabia where they sold for about $10 a piece. All efforts to obtain seedlings or cuttings were in vain, until the year 2000 when a team of British botanists succeeded in procuring a tissue culture of this rare date palm. In short, thanks to the British, saplings arrived in Israel about 10 years ago and were planted in the Beit She'an Valley, where our highest quality dates are grown. Since the dates can now be harvested, the rabbis are very excited because many halachic discussions in the Mishnah will be clarified.

A week and a half ago we celebrated Tu B'Shvat, which is also called Rosh HaShanah La-ilanot (the New Year for Trees). The use of the word *ilan* for tree is Mishnaic. The biblical term, which we use today for tree, or wood, is *eitz*. A famous rabbi, Yochanan ben Zakai (who lived about 2,000 years ago), said that if one is planting a tree and someone comes to tell you, "Stop, the *mashiach* is coming," one should continue planting and then go to greet the *mashiach*.

The Mishnah, in Tractate *Rosh HaShanah*, states that Tu B'Shvat is the New Year for Trees with regard to *orlah*. The fruits from a tree during its first three years of growth are considered *orlah* and may not be eaten. Tu B'Shvat terminates the third year (even though three full years have not elapsed) and ushers in the fourth year when the fruits may be eaten. However, the tree must be planted by the end of Tu B'Av in order to qualify for this transformation to its second year with the coming of Tu B'Shvat. This is because during its first few months it is considered a sapling and not yet a tree. By planting 44 days before Rosh HaShanah, the young sapling enters its second year as a tree on Tu B'Shvat. By the third Tu B'Shvat, the tree's produce is no longer *orlah*. The reason Tu B'Shvat was designated as the New Year for Trees is that by then most of the year's rain has fallen already, making it the natural start of the fruiting season.

My granddaughter Tovah and her husband, Shaul, ate 40 kinds of fruit on this holiday last week. The Tu B'Shvat seder, which Sephardim have celebrated for many years, is becoming popular here now among Ashkenazim as well.

Interestingly, the Knesset, created in 1949, celebrates its birthday on Tu B'Shvat.

Motzaei Shabbat, March 03, 2012

A long time ago I read the book *Life Is with People* by Mark Zborowski and Elizabeth Herzog. The book depicts Jewish life some time ago in the European shtetl. I have written earlier that many Chareidim tend not to go to events such as concerts and lectures, unless there is separate seating for men and women and the topic is appropriate for them. On the other hand, there is a plethora of social opportunities at familial ritual occasions. Indeed, within four days I attended two weddings and a *brit*. These clusters of events happen quite often, evoking memories of *Life Is with People*.

Purim will be soon upon us and we Jerusalemites celebrate on a different day from most of the world, so the holiday is somewhat extended for us. Taanit Esther is on the same day for all, the 13th of Adar. Purim worldwide is on the 14th, and the next day, 15th Adar, is Jerusalem's Shushan Purim. Children have vacation from school on all three days. I hope to join my family in B'nei Brak for their special Purim *seudah* on Thursday and return to Jerusalem in the evening to celebrate my own Purim the next day. At one of my *shiurim* the rabbi termed Pesach the holiday of fours – four sons, four questions, four cups of wine, four expressions of redemption. But Purim has its own fours—the Hebrew letter *mem* begins each phrase identifying a different halachah: **m**ishloach manot, **M**egillah, **m**atanot l'evyonim, and **m**ishteh.

However, my grandson Simcha has already been preparing for Pesach. Some people like to prepare their own matzot, as this way they can ensure absolute kashrut. This custom is mentioned by the classic commentators as being the ideal. Simcha joined a *chabura* (group) and together they turn the carefully watched wheat from grain kernels into the finished product – round, crisp matzot.

In the neighborhood of Meah Shearim there are various special bakeries, specifically designed for baking matzot. Simcha was very involved, starting with laboriously grinding the kernels using a hand mill. Over the next few days the flour was sifted, and the following week the *chabura* got together to bake the matzot. The flour and water are kept totally separate until the timer is started, at which point they are mixed in precise measurements, kneaded, rolled and baked – all in strictly less than 18 minutes. Each batch produces around 120 matzot, although some are disqualified due to folds or other problems in the process, which would render them *chametz*. Then, all the surfaces are cleaned and the rolling pins washed, to ensure that no dough is transferred from one batch to the next, as that would introduce some leavening into the process. This procedure was repeated about 10 times, resulting in about 70 kilos of matzah. These matzot are expensive, but Simcha bought a box to bring home to London for the holiday. Parenthetically, the entire month of Nissan, in which Pesach falls, is the longest vacation of the yeshiva year.

More Ephraim Kishon:
- Israel is a country surrounded on all sides by enemies, but the people's headaches are caused by the neighbors upstairs.
- Israel is the only country in the world where one is unlikely to dig a cellar without hitting ancient archaeological artifacts.
- Israel is the only country in the world where patients visiting physicians end up giving the doctor advice.
- Israel is the only country in the world where people read English, write Hebrew, and joke in Yiddish.
- Israel is the only country in the world where Muslims sell holy memorabilia to Christians and get paid in Jewish currency.

WEDNESDAY, MARCH 21, 2012

I can see that Purim is celebrated, unofficially, about four days in Jerusalem. On the day before the Fast of Esther, all the children up to bar/bat mitzvah age wear their costumes to school. These are often unusually clever. I've seen scarecrows, tea tables, an aquarium, and a sea diver, to name a few. Since one never sees children dress up as *Levi'im* on Purim, though many dress up as *kohanim*, my grandchildren researched the clothing of the *Levi'im* during the time of the *Beit HaMikdash*. They concluded that although the Torah describes the *kohanim's* clothing in detail, the *Levi'im* are left out. With some more probing they found that the *Levi'im* dressed just like any other male during Temple times, almost 3,000 years ago. They wore a type of long dress with a coat, open in front, of a color which they could choose; a scarf on the head and a scarf at the waist with tzitzit (ritual fringes) on top; a leather yarmulke on the head; and *tefillin* on the head and on the hand. Since they wore the *tefillin* all day, the hand one was not wrapped around the fingers.

Our mayor, Nir Barkat, is an avid runner and has introduced a new event in Jerusalem. The streets were festooned with prominent signs advertising the upcoming marathon, which took place last Friday on many of the main streets in the city. These streets were cordoned off for the runners from 6:00 a.m. to about 2:00 p.m. Many participants came from other countries to compete, and this year someone from Kenya won the race.

Perhaps it's because my apartment is on the third floor; perhaps because I have some leisure time; or perhaps because Jerusalem is on a mountain top and my neighborhood is one of the highest points in the city, I find myself occasionally engrossed in skygazing when I enjoy the brilliant blue skies, the sometime cloud configurations, and the rare hazy views. Or perhaps I feel that Jerusalem is closer to heaven than any place I have ever been. There is a well-known expression – *Yerushalayim shel ma'alah ve-Yerushalayim shel matah* (The heavenly Jerusalem and the earthly Jerusalem) – that resonates with me.

Recently, I attended a concert that was very entertaining and exciting. There was a large orchestra with a number of talented opera singers performing solo and in groups. The exciting aspect of the event was that now, with the mayor's encouragement consistent with his goal of increasing cultural opportunities in Jerusalem, this was a seminal evening in starting the formation of a Jerusalem opera company. I have been to Tel Aviv several times to see that city's opera in their impressive opera house; but now, I was pleased to be a participant (by my donation) in the founding of our own opera company.

We've had a sad week, as within a span of eight days, two *Gedolei Hador* (great Torah sages and leaders) have died – the Vizhnitzer Rebbe at 96, and Rabbi Chaim Pinchas Sheinberg at 101. The Vizhnitzer Rebbe was based in B'nei Brak but had Chassidim worldwide. Rabbi Sheinberg, a Litvish (Lithuanian) rabbi, actually born and raised in the U.S., was the founder and head of the large Torah Ohr Yeshiva in Jerusalem, where he lectured until recently.

All the media here are reporting details of the tragic murder of some school children and their father, in France. Most are being buried here. This event really affected me. My *ulpan* had met at Yad Vashem not far from my home. We had an excellent four-hour tour of the large museum, although we only saw a small section of the campus, a vast area with many buildings.

It was a mind-boggling, consciousness-raising, heart-wrenchingly sad experience. Upon exiting, we learned the news of the anti-Semitic outrage that occurred in France. It seems as if some things never change.

May we have only happy news to report to one another and may we pray for peace for our people and for all nations.

Wednesday, April 18, 2012

Upon my return from a very happy family Pesach celebration in London, I noticed that the city street lamps were still decorated with banners proclaiming *Chag Cheirut Sameach* – "Happy Holiday of Freedom." Chag HaCheirut is one of the four names of Pesach. The biblical name is Chag HaMatzot, and the other two names are Chag HaAviv and, of course, Chag HaPesach.

Several friends brought up the subject of the recent pro-Palestinian demonstrators from Europe who arrived to de-legitimize the State of Israel. I learned that over 2,000 were scheduled to arrive, but most European countries cooperated with Israel and the majority was stopped from boarding their Israel-bound flights at European airports including Manchester, Brussels and Paris. However, some provocateurs did arrive and proceeded to attract a lot of negative attention in the media. An IDF lieutenant colonel, who for two hours was working to subdue the violence, had his hand broken by a demonstrator and he hit the man in the face with his rifle. The perpetrator sustained a minor injury on his lip while the commanding officer was whisked away for emergency surgery. He has been dismissed from his post and, although he remains in the IDF with the same rank, he will not be allowed to command troops in the field for two years. Israel is generally given very poor press by the media, which seems to have a bias against the state…but this is an old story.

How startled I was to hear the greeting *Shanah Tovah* on the radio on the 1st of Nissan! And then I remembered that there are four New Years on the Jewish calendar.

The earliest one is the 1st of Nissan. It marks the New Year for: 1) counting the years of the reigns of kings in ancient Israel; 2) determining the order of the festivals, Pesach being the first of the three; 3) the months of the year – in the Bible, Nissan is called "the first month," and the other months are counted with reference to Nissan; 4) leap years; and 5) the donation of shekalim. The latter two were relevant in the days of the Temple.

The 1st of Elul was considered the New Year for animal tithes to the priestly class in ancient Israel.

The 1st of Tishrei is the date when the Jewish calendar year advances – the first day of Rosh HaShanah – and is traditionally seen as the date when the world was created.

The 15th of Shvat celebrates the New Year for trees.

My friend was recently davening at the Kotel from 11:30 p.m. to about 1:00 a.m., and she commented on the huge numbers of people there and the many who kept arriving as she was leaving. She told me that those people who walk to the Kotel on Shabbat can get a free Egged Bus ride to the center of Jerusalem after nightfall. Of course, the buses don't arrive at the Kotel until at least 40 minutes after sundown, when the stars are out and it is permissible to ride in a motorized vehicle. The bus company is aware that people don't carry money on Shabbat and provides free transportation for them for the hour or two after Shabbat has ended. However, this free bus ride is on the honor system, and Egged asks you to pay double for your next bus ride during the week. Apparently, drivers are not surprised when you say you needed the free ride from the Kotel after Shabbat and that's why you are paying double for your first weekday ride. In addition, coffee and cake are provided gratis at the Kotel after *Havdalah*, when Shabbat ends!

TUESDAY, APRIL 24, 2012

This year, since Yom HaAtzmaut falls on Friday, we will be celebrating it the day before, on the 4th of Iyar instead of the 5th. Yom HaZikaron, which always falls on the day before Yom HaAtzmaut, will therefore be moved up a day, and memorial ceremonies will begin tonight. The TV station at the Knesset has been broadcasting the names of over 2,000 Jews murdered in recent years by enemy terrorists. There will be a memorial service at the Kotel tonight and of course thousands will be attending private ceremonies at the graves of their beloved. My *ulpan* teacher said that there is not a household in Israel that isn't affected by loss or doesn't know someone who is. I have two relatives and a friend, who have each lost a son in defense of the country.

Tomorrow, at nightfall, a one-minute siren will signify the end of Memorial Day and the ushering in of Independence Day. The sudden switch is jarring, yet it reflects life's paradoxes.

Har Herzl will host massive entertainment and speeches. Flags have been decorating all the homes, and official buildings display large flags running the length of the edifices. People's garments now feature the colors blue and white, and stages have been set up through the city for various Israeli folk dance troupes to display their talents. The airplanes are practicing their creative flying formations for the crowds' enjoyment. Schools will be canceled and shops closed. Even though we are in the period of the Omer—which has been designated as a time of semi-mourning—fundamentally, *Sefirat HaOmer* is a time of excited anticipation. We count the days until Shavuot, the day God gave us the gift of the Torah. Ramban (Nachmanides, a 13th-century biblical commentator) compares this period to *chol hamo'ed*, since it connects Pesach and Shavuot, our physical freedom from Egypt and our spiritual redemption. So even during these weeks of semi-mourning, we are grateful that we have the State of Israel and we celebrate the restoration of Jewish sovereignty after 1,900 years.

WEDNESDAY, MAY 16, 2012

I read that Israel is among the countries with the highest per capita consumption of produce and sweets. I have some small anecdotal evidence attesting to these facts. In most restaurants I've visited, the fresh salads are ubiquitous and plentiful. Hotels serve the famous Israeli breakfast laden with a variety of salads. Visitors here tend to comment on the quality and quantity of Israeli salad-suffused breakfasts. In addition, my Israeli grandchildren wolf down salads so the large serving bowls are empty at the end of each meal. Now, my subjective evidence for the predilection for sweets is borne out by the beverages and cakes that are de rigueur at most meetings, such as parent-teacher conferences, as well as the small kiosks available at the theater for show intermissions. At my *ulpan*, the kiosk does a brisk business between classes. In addition, since I am a frequent tea drinker, the automatic question asked when I am served is "One or two?" The reference, of course, is to teaspoons of sugar, and often the response is "three." People look at me strangely when I demur. I think I'm the only one in Israel who drinks tea without sugar or any sweetener!

On the eve of Lag BaOmer, the Egged bus company borrowed buses from other companies to ferry people from all over Israel to Mount Meron in the north. Buses leaving the Jerusalem Central Station, at the rate of 10 an hour, were filled with people traveling to pray at the grave of Rabbi Shimon Bar Yochai, or to participate in the ritual first haircutting of their three-year-old sons. Joining in with the over 200,000 visitors was my grandson Dovid who, together with some friends from his yeshiva, decided to participate in the celebration.

First, Dovid went to daven at the rabbi's grave, which is enclosed in a large stone building with a blue dome. He said the people were sweating, as were the walls. Bleachers were set up to accommodate the crowds and after some time waiting, the major bonfire was lit by the Boyaner Rebbe. Dovid described the fire as being started methodically – with clothes, then oil poured with a silver pitcher, then another layer of clothes, and more oil. Meanwhile the clarinet and drums played slow, stately music, and suddenly as the massive fire began to glow and the flames rose higher, the music became more rhythmic, bringing people to their feet. Together, they began to sing and jump and dance, while Dovid felt the bleachers shaking beneath his feet. The hordes and droves of men were packed tightly while jumping rapidly. Dovid said it was a very moving experience!

After descending from the bleachers, he and his friends visited a number of other, smaller bonfires, also tended by Chassidic rabbis. Dovid commented that davening *Mincha* and *Maariv* with hundreds of thousands together was a memorable occasion. There were a number of three-year-olds getting their first haircuts, and Dovid also took a turn in shearing one of the locks of a youngster. This is a ritual where each of a group of men takes a turn to cut. These haircuts took place in a large tent, and the little boys apparently knew what to expect and were generally well behaved. There was free food, including hot dogs, burgers and drinks. Dovid was very pleased that he went to Mount Meron. The trip is about three hours each way and buses were available all night. My grandson left Jerusalem at 2:00 p.m. and returned about 8:00 a.m. the next day. He slept most of that day.

Shavuot is fast approaching, and I learned some details about the prayer of supplication, *Tachanun*, which is part of the weekday *Shacharit* and *Mincha* services and is found in every siddur. It is omitted from the prayers on Shabbat and festive days: Pesach, Shavuot, Sukkot, Rosh Chodesh, Chanukah, Tu B'Shvat and Purim. During the month of Sivan, in which Shavuot falls, one does not say *Tachanun* from Rosh Chodesh through the 12th of the month. The reason is that the first day of Sivan is Rosh Chodesh; the 2nd of the month is when Moshe told the Israelites to prepare themselves during the following three days to receive the Torah; the 3rd, 4th and 5th days of Sivan were the *shloshet yemei hagbalah* — the three days of separation and restraint in preparation for the receiving of the Torah at Mount Sinai; and the 6th day was when the Torah was actually given. It is what we celebrate today as Shavuot. The reason *Tachanun* is omitted on the 7th, 8th, 9th, 10th, 11th and 12th days as well is that, in contrast to Pesach and Sukkot when the people had six extra days to bring the *korban chagigah* (festival offering), Shavuot is only one day. The pilgrims were therefore given an extension of six more days in which to come to Jerusalem and offer their holiday sacrifices. I think this custom is interesting. Apparently, outside of Israel, many have the *minhag* to resume saying *Tachanun* on the 14th of Sivan, not the 13th, since Shavuot is celebrated for two days.

Also, my son Rabbi Hillel commented that the produce that is defined as *shiv'at haminim*, which the Bible says are indigenous to the Land of Israel and grow very well here, consists of: barley, which ripens and is harvested around the time of Pesach; wheat, which is harvested around the time of Shavuot; and grapes, olives, dates, figs and pomegranates, which are harvested in the fall, toward the Festival of Sukkot and afterward.

I learned some facts about my city, Jerusalem. Avraham Avinu called the place (which was later to be Mount Moriah) where he sacrificed the ram instead of his son Isaac *Hashem Yir'eh* — God will see [Genesis 22:14]. King Malki-Tzedek, who is identified as Shem, the son of Noah, called the place *Shalem* — perfect, complete, whole, connecting heaven and earth, connecting people to *Hashem* and to one another. The two names were combined to form *yir'eh shalem* — He shall see its perfection. Others interpret the word *yir'eh* as meaning "awe." When the city is a place of awe and service to God, it is perfect. The two words — "awe" and "completeness" — combine to create a single wholeness.

Tuesday, June 12, 2012

The Birthright program brings many college students to Israel for an intensive and hopefully positive 10-day experience. Students from the Massachusetts Institute of Technology who participate in the program are invited to remain another few days, at the expense of the MIT Hillel, to visit many start-up computer companies and other technologically sophisticated enterprises. My great-niece, who is concluding her year of learning in a girls' seminary right near the Kotel, has been admitted to MIT and will enter in the fall. She has been invited to join the MIT Birthright students for their additional five days of learning about Israel's advanced technological business opportunities. Actually, Dalia has made other contacts in the Israeli scientific arena. Recently, she was a Shabbat guest of the Orthodox family of Minister of Science and Technology Dr. Daniel Hershkowitz.

I was asked by an American friend whether Americans in Israel will tend to vote for Obama. I read a survey recently, which concluded that a clear majority of Americans here will not vote for him. I might add that both *The Jerusalem Post* and *Hamodia*, which I read, generally are not encouraging people to vote for Obama. If the situation changes, as I understand it, I will keep in touch.

The mother of an acquaintance of mine, after gaining a Ph.D. in Biblical Studies from Bar-Ilan University, has researched and is producing food as described in the Bible. She sells various items from her home, and now there is a restaurant in Tel Aviv whose owners plan to present a Biblical Day once a month. The staff will dress in clothing as described in the Bible and will serve food from recipes provided by the above expert. Since some of the ingredients are quite rare, the restaurant's *mashgiach* needs to spend more time ascertaining the kashrut. I think this is still a work in progress.

My musical ensemble, Manginot Me-HaOlam, consisting of seven women ranging in age from 50 to 80, displays a variety of religious customs. Our flautist felt it inappropriate for us to rehearse on Yom HaAtzmaut, although the other musicians came to the rehearsal. Our singer won't sing in front of men, although she is happy to say the words of the songs while the ensemble plays. Our pianist doesn't perform in front of men. However, we are so fortunate that she is a composer and lyricist, and we introduce at least two of her works to our audiences. Our organist won't rehearse or play any gigs during the three weeks between the 17th of Tammuz and the 9th of Av. Our percussionist, as well as most of the group, won't practice during the nine days from the first of Av through Tisha B'Av. Our violinist will play and/or sing on all days before all audiences. Except for the violinist, all the musicians identify themselves as Orthodox. Despite this diversity, the group members get along really well together, and we have had some very successful gigs over the last six months. We have performed for a Yiddish club, a book launching, the Association of Americans and Canadians, and several times for senior citizens' homes or clubs. We play as a mitzvah, but our transportation is reimbursed. Some examples of our selections are: "La Paloma" (Spain); "Bulgar Freilach" (Romania); "Miserlou" (Greece); "O Sole Mio" (Italy); "Memory" (England); "Los Bilbilicos" (Ladino); "Turkey in the Straw" (America); and "Dark Eyes" (Russia). I am learning a lot about directing and am enjoying the entire experience.

Close to 30 years ago, my son Hillel spent several years learning in Kfar Chabad, a village of Lubavitcher Chassidim in the vicinity of Lod. Recently, Hillel's son Dovid, who is studying in Jerusalem this year, spent an interesting and inspiring Shabbat visiting the *kfar*. He and two friends slept in a dormitory, which houses boys from outside of Israel who are learning there. Dovid and his friends ate with a hospitable family. They enjoyed the countryside and welcoming atmosphere. The area has expanded to two sections, basically for political purposes. They are similar but independent entities and are meant to accommodate more residents and maintain Chabad control of the village. As I understand it, if the village develops into a city, the government takes over its maintenance. The *kfar* boasts several productive industries, including a matzah bakery, a honey farm, and two *etrog* orchards. Unfortunately, Dovid and his friends missed the last bus to Jerusalem, were able to get a bus to Tel Aviv, but missed the last bus from there to Jerusalem. Banking on Israeli hospitality, Dovid called a relative at 1:30 a.m. and described the situation. This host kindly invited the boys to spend the night, fed them a tasty breakfast in the morning and sent them on their way. They arrived at their yeshiva a little late for the morning davening but were able to continue their day of learning. They had a very good Shabbat and enjoyed the unplanned Tel Aviv hospitality.

TUESDAY, JULY 17, 2012

A friend sent me a list of impressive facts pertaining to Israel, a few of which I include here:

- Israel is ranked No. 2 in the world for venture capital funds right behind the U.S.;
- Outside the U.S. and Canada, Israel has the largest number of NASDAQ listed companies;
- On a per capita basis, Israel has the largest number of biotech startups;

- Twenty-four percent of Israel's workforce holds university degrees, ranking third in the industrialized world after the U.S. and Holland, and twelve percent hold advanced degrees;
- Israel is the only liberal democracy in the Middle East;
- When Golda Meir was elected Prime Minister of Israel in 1969, she became the world's second elected female leader in modern times.

I read an article by Naomi Ragen, "The Strangers Among Us," in the June 15 issue of *The Jerusalem Post*, which I think very accurately reflects the conflicting emotions of many Israelis regarding the close to 1,000 people a month from Sudan and Eritrea who have illegally inundated Israel seeking a better way of life. Most come from terrible situations in their native countries and we Israelis have compassionately empathized with them. On the other hand, the burden on the medical system, social services and demographics, to name a few, has caused a major problem here, and the government has decided to give the Eritreans some spending money and fly them back to their native lands. Ragen writes:

> *Nevertheless, I would be a hypocrite if I didn't admit to viewing with relief his [Netanyahu's] initiative not to extend the temporary residence status for asylum-seekers and to return them to their native countries.*
>
> *Israel is just too small to take in every African seeking a better life. But that doesn't mean it doesn't hurt.*

And the article concludes:

> *In the meantime, Israel is busily building a 200-kilometer barrier along the border with Egypt, which might be the most sensible long-term solution to this insoluble problem that pits our hearts against our heads, our near history against our present circumstances.*

Closer to home, if you should happen to be in the Jewish Quarter on a Thursday night, on a large deck facing the Kotel, you would be in for an informal musical treat. My grandson Dovid reported that talented boys from various yeshivot come with their instruments to play classical Jewish songs, both Hebrew and English. Dovid counted eight guitars, three bongos, two violins, three flutes, a soprano sax, a clarinet and two recorders. This ensemble, with no notes, no music stands and no chairs, entices a large group of onlookers who join in by singing the well-known tunes.

In contrast to the individual street musicians often found on street corners in the center of Jerusalem—especially on the pedestrian mall of Ben Yehuda—who appreciate donations from the onlookers, these yeshiva boys who do impromptu jamming in the vicinity of the Kotel do not solicit any contributions. The group begins at 11:00 p.m. and continues until after 2:00 a.m. An especially joyous happening! However, Dovid tells me that there is a rabbinic opinion that it is not appropriate to have instrumental music in the Kotel vicinity, since the Wall is a remnant of the Temple for which we are yearning. So far, the musicians have not been evicted! Of course, during the three weeks leading up to the Tisha B'Av fast, when we mourn the destruction of the first and second Temples, as well as other tragedies that have befallen our people, there is no instrumental music in the area. I wish my readers an easy fast.

WEDNESDAY, AUGUST 8, 2012

Since I have three 18- or 19-year-old grandchildren learning in yeshivot, I thought it would be helpful for me to know their schedules and a little bit about their learning programs. Nochum Dovid, my Israeli grandson, reports the following. Boys arise at 6:45 and daven *Shacharit*. Then they learn *parshat hashavua*, that week's Bible portion, with Rashi commentary. Next comes breakfast, which consists of bread, plain cheese, hard-boiled eggs, yogurt and salad. At 9:00 they proceed to the main morning's learning with a *chavruta* (partner). Nochum's current *masechta* (one of the 63 tractates in Gemara) is *Kiddushin*, the laws of betrothal and marriage, which he learns in depth and with many commentaries and interpretations. From 12:00 to 1:15 a rabbi lectures on the same subject, fielding questions from the 30 boys in the class. Lunch consists of plain meat, vegetables (mostly potatoes) and bread. Then they learn *Hilchot Shabbat* (laws pertaining to Shabbat), either alone or with a *chavruta*. Rest time is 2:15 to 3:30, after which the boys gather for the afternoon prayer of *Mincha*. Next, the same subject of *kiddushin* is studied, but as more of an overview, more quickly. Dinner at 7:30 consists of bread, bourekas, rice or kugel eaten, as are all the meals, in the large dining room with the entire yeshiva of 300 boys. At 8:00 there is a *musar* (moral and ethical conduct) lecture, at 9:00 the boys daven the evening prayer of *Maariv* and then review the same material they learned in the morning with a *chavruta* until 11:30 p.m. Nochum Dovid's yeshiva is typical for Israeli boys, more spartan in food and crowded in lodgings. Each boy shares a small room with three or four others.

Dovid Sholom, from London, studies in a large yeshiva building with a different floor allocated to each level of learning. His morning program is similar to Nochum Dovid's, though his breakfast includes cereal and occasional pancakes, customary for English-speaking students. Dovid often devotes his afternoon break to practicing his flute, and several times a week he comes to my home where I accompany him on the piano. Nochum Dovid, too, occasionally stops here to do his laundry and ironing. Dovid's afternoon schedule is similar to Nochum's. At various times in the early evening a lecture on *musar* is common to all the yeshivot, and all the boys daven three times daily. Dovid's yeshiva includes Americans, South Africans, Belgians and Brits, and the administration organizes for them occasional trips throughout Israel. Dovid also has a lively social life with his friends—going to beaches (separate swimming), occasionally playing soccer on Thursday or Saturday nights, and being a frequent guest at various homes for Shabbat. Dovid Sholom shares a large room with two other boys.

Simcha, a Londoner as well, learns in a similarly large yeshiva, which includes boys of various ages and learning levels. Parenthetically, it is the same yeshiva in which his father learned over 25 years ago. His learning and davening schedule is similar to that of the other boys, though he is studying a different section in the Talmud. There is the similar pattern of learning with a partner, followed by a lecture—often interactive—on the subject learned, with a review later in the day. His day continues until 11:00 p.m. Although Simcha also learns with English speakers, his yeshiva resembles Nochum's in some ways, since there are a fair amount of Hebrew speakers and the boys are typically older. However, the lodgings in Simcha's yeshiva are similar to those in Dovid Sholom's.

Nochum will probably stay in the same place until he is married. The others may be returning to London after spending a few years here. My good fortune is that they are all not far from me and come to visit, use my computer, and have a nosh or two. By the way, the Friday schedules continue only through the morning, so the boys can shop, travel to their Shabbat destinations, visit friends, and come to wish me *A Guten Shabbos*.

Three weeks ago, a Gadol HaDor, the venerable head of the Chareidi yeshiva world passed away. Several hours after his death, close to 300,000 people accompanied the deceased to his resting place. Since the roads were closed to vehicular traffic and filled with mourners, nearby residents were able to stand on corners and on rooftops, joining the masses in mourning the demise of Rabbi Yosef Shalom Elyashiv. My daughter-in-law Ruthie, visiting from London, was among the mourners. There are many inspirational anecdotes about this brilliant Torah scholar. Two brief items I heard from my grandson Nochum Dovid: When the rav (rabbi or teacher) was asked any type of question, he responded immediately, and so clearly and precisely that there could be no misinterpretation of his words. He answered halachic questions from around the world, including one about the status of spouses of the dead in the U.S. 9/11 attacks. (There have to be witnesses to a death in order that a spouse may halachically remarry.) I excerpt a few paragraphs from my son Rabbi Rashi's shul publication:

> *Rav Elyashiv, renowned for his breathtaking hasmadah [diligence in Torah study] and absolute command of the entire Torah literature, held no official position, yet was the final word in Jewish law for hundreds of thousands of Orthodox Jews across the world. His daily lecture in a local shul, delivered for nearly 80 years, was an astounding tapestry of topics across the Talmud Bavli and Yerushalmi, halachah and aggadah...*

Rav Elyashiv was an only child born 17 years after his parents' marriage. He married the daughter of the famous Reb Aryeh Levin, "the tzaddik of Jerusalem," renowned for his extraordinary acts of *chesed*, such as visiting prisoners and leper colonies. The match was proposed by the great Rabbi Avraham Kook, who also performed the couple's wedding. They had 12 children, 10 of whom reached adulthood. Their daughters went on to marry prominent rabbinic scholars, and their sons became well-known rabbis. Rav Elyashiv merited the unique experience of having all his grandchildren marry in his lifetime, and even more remarkable, in 2009, his great-grandson became a grandfather. He lived to see almost 1,000 direct descendants. May his memory be for a blessing.

SUNDAY, AUGUST 19, 2012

As I had planned to spend this summer at home in Jerusalem, the highlight having been the birth of my third great-grandson with the attendant *brit* and the impending *pidyon haben*, it seemed a good idea to give myself a one-day treat out of the ordinary routine. Some friends recommended a *tiyul* to the area near Alon Shvut and the ancient city of Chevron. My bus held the standard 40 people who were a very comradely group. Although walking and stair climbing don't come easily to me, with the help of fellow travelers and my trusty cane, I did very well. I'd like to report only a miniscule amount of the plethora of information imparted by our very knowledgeable and eloquent guide:

In Chevron I saw the oldest staircase in the world. These were the steps that Avraham Avinu climbed, leading to the city gate where he met Ephron, the Hittite. Avraham had just returned from the *Akeidah*, the near-sacrifice of his son Isaac, and purchased his wife Sarah's grave for 400 talents of silver paid to Ephron. We visited the cave of the graves of our forefathers and foremothers, called Ma'arat HaMachpela, and we had the opportunity to daven in that holy place. The question, for which the answer remains speculative, is: from where did Avraham get the silver? One response is that it was known that the Plishtim came from over the Aegean Sea and had brought the silver, which Avraham, who was a rich man, had acquired by bartering with them. Most business affairs in those days were conducted at the city gate, and we did see a massive gate of rock stretching 25 feet in width, which is said to be that city gate. In biblical times, city gates were the center of city life, and our literature often describes the elders and other important officials as "sitting at the gate." For example, Boaz went to the town gate looking for Naomi's next of kin to ask for the right to marry Ruth. King Herod built the building above the cave over 2,000 years ago, on bedrock, with the same giant stones he used for building the Kotel.

Not far from the same area, we came across milestones erected during the Roman occupation. Set at intervals on an ancient main road are huge stone pillars, with traces of gold paint, which list the number of miles to the next city. Our guide said that there are more of these pillars in Israel than in any other place except for Italy. And finally, we saw an unusual *mikveh* built in the first century B.C.E.

Three factors distinguished this *mikveh* from others. First, it was facing vast fields of farmland. Second, its water supply was an amazing tour de force. Rainwater was gathered in a nearby hill and transferred by means of underground pipes to this depression in the ground called a *mikveh*. Our guide said that since women in ancient days were generally pregnant or nursing, the *mikvaot* were mainly used by men. Now, here comes the third unusual aspect of this *mikveh*. It had an entrance and an exit. The area was inhabited by the tribe of Yehuda, who mainly cultivated vineyards. The men who harvested the grapes during the special season of the *batzir* (biblical word meaning "grape harvest") had to immerse in the *mikveh* before harvesting. Since this *mikveh* had two apertures, the overseer was able to observe the men who placed their dirty clothes near one door, entered the *mikveh*, and exited by the adjacent door where they put on their clean clothes.

These are mere fragments of all the information imparted, so you can see that I found the *tiyul* interesting and informative, and gained a renewed appreciation of our biblical heritage.

As I mentioned, I was anticipating celebrating the *pidyon haben* of my great-grandson Yitzchok. Though the mitzvah of *pidyon haben* is referred to several times in the Torah, it is statistically an uncommon ritual due to various conditions. The festive celebration was held in a comfortable hall with colorfully decorated tables, which later featured a tasty formal meal. The atmosphere was joyful as the friends and family from near and far, throughout Israel and even London, enjoyed the opportunity to witness the redemption of the month-old baby Yitzchok—whose parents were not *kohanim* or *Levi'im*—from a well-known Jerusalem *kohein*. In my 45 years of residing in Lafayette I remember attending only two, or maybe three, *pidyon haben* ceremonies. Some of my seasoned friends may remember the event that Ed and I hosted 26 years ago for the redemption of my first grandson. Saadia was redeemed by (until recently) Purdue's only Nobel Prize winner, *kohein* and chemistry professor, Herb Brown, ably assisted by his wife, Sarah, who transliterated the proper ritual phrases.

Something very touching about today's occasion relates to the following story. During the Holocaust, a wealthy family gave their son to a non-Jewish neighbor, with funds for his upkeep. The parents survived the terror, but their young son didn't. They dedicated a very beautiful, large, silver tray with an inscription in memory of their son and donated it to a *gemach*. Now, baby Yitzchok was placed upon this tray—which was decorated with jewelry lent by the women guests—and then presented to the *kohein* to be redeemed. *Mazal Tov* to the family!

If you like to read history, you'll enjoy a new book, *Herod – The Man Who Had to be King*, by Yehuda Shulewitz. His wife, Malka, a dear friend of mine, had the book published posthumously, with her "finishing touches." She wrote me that this book has the honor of being the first fictional account of the Herodian period, set in the whole of the Mediterranean area. Friends who have purchased it said that for them it makes the many characters of that sometimes tragic but interesting era come to life. Mordechai Nisan, a critic, writes:

> *Yehuda Shulewitz wrote a historical novel of a dazzling and vicious historical personality. We do not easily know if the conventional historical record of Herod and his times is accurate: there are questions concerning the famous work The Wars of the Jews by Joseph Flavius (Yosef ben Matityahu).... This fictional work may be markedly more accurate by plumbing the depths of Herod's soul.*

I'm now partway through reading this meticulously researched historical novel published by Penina Press.

In Lafayette, over 50 years ago, I founded the Hadassah Study Group. This activity gave me and a number of other women a chance to read and discuss many books on Jewish subjects. I am so pleased to say that National Hadassah gave our group several awards, including third best in the nation. We were in competition with some 300 study groups. About a year ago, I was invited to join a similar program here. There are several differences in the format; for instance, this group confines its reading to fiction on Jewish subjects. Nevertheless, the 9 or 10 attendees are bright and eloquent, so I find the experience rewarding. Some recent book reviews include *The Invisible Bridge*, *The Dream of Scipio* and *Sarah's Key*.

The background of this group of women reveals some Israeli history. A talented Hebrew University professor of English literature, Shulamit Nardi, upon her retirement over 15 years ago, invited several students to gather informally at her home to continue reading and reviewing fiction on Jewish subjects in English. When she died in 2002, the (by then) mature women decided to maintain her program. I once had a personal encounter with Mrs. Nardi. Many years ago, when I visited the president's home with a group of academics, she met and graciously hosted us. I have since learned that she served as an advisor to five presidents of Israel—from Zalman Shazar (third president) to Ezer Weizman (seventh president)—until 1995, just seven years before she died at the age of 93. She also served as chief translator and speech writer at the President's Residence. I remember her as a lovely and modest lady.

Sunday, September 9, 2012

Although the Lafayette community is likely familiar with the Birthright program, since Purdue's Hillel director has been leading groups of students to Israel for some 10 years, my other readers may be interested in a few details I gleaned from my grandson Saadia. He recently spent 10 days in Israel in charge of a busload of college students aged 18 to 26. He told me of his thorough preparation, including reading the applications of all participants so he would be familiar with them. He said that this summer there had been a backlog of 5,000 students who wanted to be part of Birthright (in Israel known as Taglit, the Hebrew word for discovery, or revelation). A wealthy donor, Sheldon Adelson, who had contributed $20 million to the program, added another $13 million to reduce the waiting line. So, with three weeks' notice, Saadia and his charges were on their way!

Organizers estimate that they will have brought 42,000 people to Israel within the year. As reported in *The Jerusalem Post*, a poll revealed that although middle-agers in the U.S. are not as supportive of Israel as their parents' generation, their teenage children are much more pro-Israel. The poll attributes this phenomenon to the Birthright program.

In addition to traveling the length and breadth of the country, the participants had time for discussions and evaluations. Each bus had an Israeli tour guide and another Israeli to answer any specific detailed questions. Of course, an armed soldier accompanied the group, and several more soldiers joined for a day to provide an opportunity for Israelis and Americans to become better acquainted. A number of organizations are affiliated with the Birthright program. The Orthodox Union, the one with which Saadia is connected, offers interested participants the choice of being with a completely *shomer Shabbat* (Sabbath observant) group.

This summer, in addition to celebrating my great-grandon's *brit mila* and then his *pidyon haben* – events that brought Rashi and his family here for some time – I hosted Hillel's 15-year-old son, Mendy, for three weeks. While his brother Dovid was on vacation from yeshiva, the boys visited old shuls in Tzfat and the graves of famous rabbis. They also swam in the Mediterranean near Netanya. After Dovid returned to his studies, Mendy had a chance to explore two of the four interesting sites that are within walking distance from my home. Although he didn't stroll through the military cemetery, or the beautiful Jerusalem Forest, he did spend a meaningful afternoon at Yad Vashem. What made a sobering impression on him was the room where the millions of children killed in the Holocaust were each named and symbolized by a small, brightly lit bulb. Mendy also walked to Har Herzl, where during the one-hour tour of the museum he learned a great deal about the founder of the State of Israel.

Together with my other London grandchildren Elisheva and Yehuda, Mendy and I found the visit to the Menachem Begin Heritage Center well worthwhile. Begin's values, strong leadership and oratory skills, as well as his being a recipient with Sadat of the Nobel Peace Prize, were all very skillfully portrayed. The three grandchildren and I also visited our foremother Rachel's grave. It is on the outskirts of Bethlehem, about a 50-minute bus ride from the center of Jerusalem. Somewhat daunting is a very high, gray stone wall housing an army compound, assuring the safety of the pilgrims to the area. The cozy women's section, with a full view of the tomb, was filled with people beseeching "Mameh Rochel" for help. She is typically known as crying for her children to return to their homeland. Often, the thin red string worn on the wrist, which is known to have some kabbalistic significance, is sold here for some *tzedakah*.

A friend of mine is a docent at the Jerusalem Bible Lands Museum, and I recently joined one of her tours learning about the pure, exquisite, golden treasures of the ancient world. The museum featured priceless jewelry and vessels from Mesopotamia, Persia, the Baltic Sea Region and China. I hope to return to enjoy the video descriptions expanding on many details of the rare and astonishing exhibits.

Monday, September 10, 2012

To meet with the secular crowd, perhaps hippies and assorted characters, singers and musicians, the place to be is the Ben Yehuda pedestrian mall on Thursday nights. I learned of a pub nightclub limited to men from the yeshiva crowd only, not far from Ben Yehuda. My grandson went there with a couple of friends; the drinks were reasonably priced, probably mainly beer, and there was a combo playing familiar Chassidic songs. Dovid stayed until about 3:00 a.m. and was able to hitch a ride back to his yeshiva. Another meeting place is the Kotel. After you finish davening, you may likely encounter someone you know, though these would tend to be the religious types. There are options here for all tastes.

Rosh HaShanah is in the air! Impromptu kiosks abound, selling *kartisay bracha* for the holidays ("Shanah Tovah" cards), honey cake and round sweet challot; large, decorated baskets of wine, honey, olive oil and chocolates are on sale; newspapers are filled with ads for new furniture and other household items. All these, and daily shofar blowing throughout the month of Elul, sensitize us to the impending Days of Judgment. Even at the dentist's office, small jars of honey are given out to clients! Throughout Elul we are encouraged to reexamine our relationships with our fellow man, with *Hashem* and with ourselves. This month of introspection should motivate us to improve ourselves by attempting to rectify our errors.

Friday, September 28, 2012

The verve and joy of the Sukkot holiday are readily apparent, and Jerusalem is transformed. Traditionally, the first nail is placed in the sukkah directly after breaking the fast of Yom Kippur. All around me there is hammering, and I rather like it because it heralds a very happy time, Zman Simchateinu. Sukkot are springing up like mushrooms, on balconies and rooftops, in front and in back of buildings. Many families have their own sukkah; some even have two, one for eating and one for sleeping. A family of new *olim* had their sukkah gifted to them by their landlord, who told them the first mitzvah is to have a sukkah and the second is to make aliyah. Colorful stands abound, with boys selling pretty and meaningful decorations, including posters of famous rabbis and of the *ushpizin*. One street is cordoned off and all vehicles, including buses, are diverted to an alternate route because there is a lively crowd surrounding the many long tables where each customer is choosing his special *lulav* and *etrog*. I have a small sukkah on my porch and am looking forward to entertaining in it. I also have invitations, as always, for Shabbat meals, and now for holiday meals as well. Here, we only celebrate one day *Yom Tov*, so there is a longer *chol hamo'ed*.

With the arrival of my grandson Yechiel from Milwaukee, I now have a teenage boy from each of my children learning Torah here. Yechiel is part of a Modern Orthodox program based at Bar-Ilan University. He has already visited the graves of our sages in Tiberias, done rock climbing, and gone rafting and tubing on the Kinneret. The main part of his program includes an *ulpan* for learning conversational Hebrew, classes in Jewish history, philosophy, ethics, Bible and some Talmud. Yesterday, I had an unexpected 1:30 a.m. call from Yechiel asking if he could sleep here. His group had come to Yerushalayim to daven at the Kotel with an estimated 250,000 others saying *Slichot* during the Days of Awe between Rosh HaShanah and Yom Kippur. In the morning he continued on to B'nei Brak to spend Yom Kippur with his Aunt Shira and family.

And now, here is some family news. This Chol HaMo'ed Sukkot will be six years since my husband died. My granddaughter Yocheved has been editing his voluminous papers and, with some input from me and a cover design by my granddaughter Brocha, the book is now at the printer. Hopefully, it will be ready for distribution on Ed's imminent *yahrtzeit*. In addition to family, I hope to give it to some interested friends.

I was fortunate to have spent Shabbat and Rosh HaShanah in London. Among many informative and edifying remarks from my children, I learned that around the year 300 C.E. Rabbi Abahu, who was a wealthy merchant and statesman living in Caesarea (the Roman capital of occupied Israel in its day), instituted the order and manner of the shofar sounds as well as the wording of the prayers surrounding the shofar blowing as we do it today. Maimonides notes that from the biblical imperative to sound the *truah*, it is uncertain if it refers to *anachah*, a groaning cry, which is what we call *shvarim*, or to *yelalah*, a wailing cry, which is what we call *truah*. For many years there were two traditions, until Rabbi Abahu codified our practice of sounding these two separate shofar notes and then blowing them together to fulfill the mitzvah of *truah*.

Some family *naches* includes: Hillel, who supervises the kashrut at the royal banquets in London, was widely quoted in the fall issue of the magazine *Kosher Spirit* (circulation 100,000) where he described the queen's kosher dinnerware and how the entire palace kitchen is *kashered* (made kosher) for certain occasions.

Motzaei Shabbat, October 6, 2012

A palpable sense of happiness during the Sukkot holiday is created by nighttime music and dancing at many yeshivot. President Shimon Peres hosted thousands of visitors in his immense sukkah. I was told that people stood in line outside with police guaranteeing orderly conduct. Throughout the holiday, people from all over the country come to Jerusalem and make their way on foot to the holy Kotel. In this way, they follow in the footsteps of their ancestors who, in ancient times, would fulfill the obligation to be *oleh regel* (literally, "going up on foot"), bringing their sacrifices to the *Beit HaMikdash* on the three pilgrimage festivals – Pesach, Shavuot and Sukkot. On the second *chol hamo'ed* day, hundreds of thousands of people made their way to the Kotel, hoping to witness and hear *Birkat Kohanim*. The following day, the streets downtown were cordoned off to vehicular traffic for the annual Jerusalem March, a festive parade that winds through town and attracts participants from all over Israel and around the world. Another aspect of the holiday, which I enjoy, is the *Mo'adim LeSimcha* greeting that prefaces each of the news broadcasts.

My grandson Yechiel's program seems very effective in taking advantage of so many of the special opportunities here. One group activity consisted of filling and personally delivering 200 bags with treats and small gifts to children hospitalized in the pediatric ward of Israel's largest hospital, the Sheba Medical Center, also known as Tel HaShomer Hospital since it's located in the Tel HaShomer area of Ramat Gan. I recently learned that the group went to B'nei Brak to dance in the Simchat Beit HaShoeva celebrations, which take place every evening during Chol HaMo'ed Sukkot. This activity is primarily done by boys, but sometimes an area is cordoned off for the girls to dance as well. It is fun to watch the lively frolicking and leaping.

Although I have been to the Bible Lands Museum a number of times, I didn't realize that there was a large backyard. I attended a bar mitzvah celebration there, in a gigantic sukkah. There was excellent amplification and the bar mitzvah spoke eloquently and in depth, focusing on aspects of the Sukkot holiday. The hundreds of guests were fashionably attired. There was copious food and the table centerpieces consisted of stalks of grain and attractive produce arrangements. The band was talented and led by a former rock star who had become religious. Sporting a long beard, he was dressed in a kaftan and strummed the guitar. Except for a number of well-known local rabbis, everyone spoke in English. It subsequently became clear to me that while my host lives in London and is a member of Rashi's shul, he owns an apartment in Herzliya to which he and his family repair several times a year. Many of the British guests spend part of the year in their Israel apartments. Quite a nice arrangement, I think.

Thursday, October 25, 2012

I welcomed my friend from New Jersey to the 6th *yahrtzeit* commemoration for Ed. She grew up in the same neighborhood as Ed and joined 23 family members around my table as she recollected memories of Ed's childhood. My family then read aloud some of his correspondence with his grandchildren. My friend and I met over 60 years ago in Elizabeth, New Jersey, when we were members of a Young Judaea Club with a special emphasis on Israeli folk dancing. Actually, one of the primary purposes of her visit was to be a delegate to the Hadassah Centennial Convention. She spoke enthusiastically about the well-planned and thrilling program, including the opportunity to witness the dedication of the Davidson Tower, endowed by New York's Mayor Bloomberg; an exciting hike down into the Old City's City of David; and the experience of the instant camaraderie and *ruach* of the delegates. Some statistics regarding the convention include: 1900 delegates from 40 states and 13 countries with 600 male Hadassah associates in attendance.

Recently, I learned some new words and expressions. The word for postage stamp is *bul*; but *bul* has an additional meaning – "right to the point," or "precisely." An arrow hitting its target exactly is called – *bul pegi'ah* taken from the English "bull's eye," and *pegi'ah* meaning "a hit," not to be confused with the word *pagiya*, which means "a premature baby." I also learned that on the holiday of Hoshana Rabbah, people wish each other *a guten kvittel* (in Yiddish), or *pitka tava* (in Aramaic), or the Hebraized *pitkah tovah*. The final sealing of a person's yearly judgment occurs on Hoshana Rabbah, and these expressions mean that at this last opportunity, may you be inscribed for a good year. Another new expression is used after Simchat Torah, when people wish one another *choref bari*, "a healthy winter," which is Yiddishized to "*a guten vinter.*" I thought this was rather strange since the weather was still hot here and we were in mid-October. But my son-in-law Shlomo reminded me that there are really only two seasons here—the dry and the wet—and since we pray for rain on Shmini Atzeret, and continue the request in the daily *Shmoneh Esreih* prayer until Pesach, we are anticipating the rainy season, which in Israel denotes winter.

The yeshiva world has its own jargon. Here are some examples:
- *ram* – acronym for *rosh mesivtah* – gives the daily lecture covering the material learned in the morning with a study partner;
- *rosh yeshiva* – the head of a yeshiva;

- *mazkir* (male) or *mazkirah* (female) – office administrator;
- *mashgiach* – makes sure the students attend all sessions, generally checks on their behavior, and gets help for them if they are ill;
- *menahel ha-binyan*, or *av bayit* – the person responsible for the physical premises.

The high school boys call their teacher Rebbi or HaRav; the girls call all their teachers HaMorah if it's a woman and HaRav if it's a man. A female kindergarten teacher is called a *ganenet*, while her male counterpart is a *ganan*, or *ganan yeladim*. Although the girls remain in kindergarten until age 5, the boys begin *cheider* at age 3.

The son-in-law of a dear friend, whose family I visited on Sukkot, is a *dayan*, a judge in a rabbinical court, in Ashkelon. There are two court systems in Israel – the secular and the religious, or rabbinical, courts. He answered my several questions about the latter. The purview of these religious courts includes marriage, divorce, conversion and child abuse. In most cases, if the man wants the divorce it is because he has found another woman. If the woman sues for divorce it is often because the man is abusive. In that case, if the man is uncooperative, his home can be taken from him; then his license can be confiscated; he may be barred from dealing with any banks; and finally, he can be put in jail. "Our sympathies are always with the woman," said this judge. The court sees cases where there are serious problems with children and has at its disposal a cadre of social workers and psychologists. There are 10 rabbinical courts throughout the country with a total of 90 judges who all know one another and work together when necessary. The High Court is in Jerusalem. I enjoyed a stimulating and meaningful Sukkot visit with my friend and her family.

Since there were some rockets fired on Ashkelon this morning, causing several injuries – some serious – I will close with prayers for peace in Israel and the world.

Friday, October 26, 2012

My grandson Yechiel regales me with details of his *tiyulim* in Israel. He recently learned, on an archeological dig, about the glass, copper, pottery, bone, and metal finds in Jerusalem. The knowledgeable archeologist pointed out that various eras are reflected by a defining shape of the finds. His group also enjoyed the experience of wading hip-high in water in Chizkiyahu's

Tunnel. Chizkiyahu was king of Judah from approximately 715 to 686 B.C.E. Yechiel has also visited a number of museums throughout Israel, including the 3-year-old Rambam Museum in Tiberias—featuring the life and legacy of Maimonides—and the Yitzchak Rabin museum in Tel Aviv. His program, called The Israel Experience, unfortunately included the funeral of the mother of their *av bayit*.

Yechiel was startled by the different funeral customs in Israel as compared to those in the United States.

Monday, November 19, 2012

As I commence my letter with a review of some happy events of the last several weeks, our part of the world is clouded over by news of hundreds of rockets raining down on primarily, but not solely, the southern part of our country, causing many injuries and some tragic deaths. Today, several friends told me that their sons and those of many neighbors have been called up to the army. A great many young men from the religious yeshivot have been mobilized, which leads me to think that if a cease-fire is not reached there will be massive retribution from Israel. My friend said that while the yearly call-up to *miluim* (army reserve duty for about 20-30 days) is usually by mail, the call to mobilize is generally about 6:00 a.m., with a knock on the door and orders to report to the base immediately. We pray for peace to reign.

Only 10 times a year are Jews allowed to pray in the entire area of the graves of our patriarchs and matriarchs in Chevron, and the Shabbat when the Torah portion *Chayei Sarah* is read is one of those occasions. The Islamic Waqf (Religious Trust) controls 81 percent of the site, and all other days Jews may enter only two of the three rooms – one where Abraham and Sarah are buried, and the other where Jacob and Leah lie. That particular Shabbat, the third and largest room, Isaac and Rebecca's, was opened as well. An estimated 20,000 visitors set up tents, brought their own food supplies and davened at the entire gravesite. On foot, many toured the whole scenic area, including the nearby town of Kiryat Arba. It was a real happening because people from several different streams of Judaism assembled their own minyanim and picnicked in an intensely communal environment. My grandson Yechiel, who with his group experienced this special Shabbat, told me he slept under the stars, as did our forefather Jacob. His school provided its own chef, and large portable bathrooms were set up with some privacy for changing clothes.

He reported that there were triple the number of soldiers that usually guard the area, where now only three percent of the city's residents are Jewish. Yechiel enjoyed the spirited singing that filled the air and said that the section where our forefathers are buried smelled like Gan Eden (the Garden of Eden). Since Shabbat starts so early now, about 4:00 p.m., the school provided a bus for the students to arrive, but they returned by public bus, via Jerusalem—as my 18-year-old grandson put it—"making a night of it." The experience in Chevron was meaningful, moving and spiritually uplifting, and Yechiel returned to school very excited about it.

I am generally very impressed with the Bar-Ilan program. Recently the students toured the Begin Museum in Jerusalem, which I have visited several times and would recommend highly to my readers. In addition, Yechiel has chosen to take an advocacy course, which will enable him to defend Israel, if need be, on his future college campus.

There is an extraordinary jewel of a movie, in Hebrew with English subtitles, called *Le-malei et Ha-chalal* (*Fill the Void*). It is written and directed by Rama Burshtein, an Israeli Chareidi woman who depicts so artfully some events in the life of a Chareidi family. The scenes are understated and require the viewer's full attention. The acting is outstanding, with effective facial expression and body language. The film has already won a number of awards in Europe and, according to *The Jerusalem Post*, may be nominated for an Oscar. I recommend it highly.

I was privileged to enjoy a very talented Russian troupe's rendition of Tchaikovsky's ballet *Swan Lake*. On another evening, I viewed on widescreen TV a CD presentation with commentary of a Tchaikovsky opera *Pique Dame* (*Queen of Spades*). Topping off this culturally rich week was an outing with a friend to a vocal concert of Vivaldi, Handel, Delibes and others, combined with a vast and impressive art exhibition of stunning handmade quilts, with Jerusalem as their theme.

The week's events also included a delightful birthday party for my 14-year-old granddaughter in B'nei Brak which, since it was Rosh Chodesh Kislev, featured *sufganiyot*, a reminder that Chanukah is not far off.

My musical ensemble will be performing at two Chanukah celebrations including, for the first time, an appearance in B'nei Brak. We were told that no group such as ours exists there. I am especially proud of our international Chanukah songs, some of which I'm sure will be sing-a-longs. We feature a variety of tunes including several in Yiddish, Ladino, Hebrew and English, familiar to most of the audience. We had to learn some new favorite Israeli melodies, different from my American Chanukah melodies.

Here is some news you may have missed from *The Jerusalem Post*:

> While exit polls show Romney received 85% of the Jewish vote from Israel, America went completely the other way. The latest figures suggest that 70% of American Jewry stuck with Obama. This is a staggering statistic. It suggests that we are on totally different wavelengths, our peoples separated by much more than an ocean and several time zones.

From *Hamodia*:

> Israel is the second most educated country in the world, says a report released by the Organization for Economic Cooperation and Development. According to the OECD's Education at a Glance 2011 report, 78% of the money invested in education in Israel is taken directly from public funds, while 45% of Israel's population has some sort of advanced training. Israel also had the largest increase in overall population, approximately 19.02% from 2000 to 2009.

My grandson Simcha recently spent part of a Shabbat in Jerusalem's Old City. He and about 40 soldiers were guests of a wealthy and generous couple, Aba and Pamela Claman who, with a large home and a staff of helpers, often entertain soldiers on Shabbat. Sometimes the army sends them an entire unit. Some soldiers sleep at the Clamans' home, and accommodations are found for the others. Part of the joy of that Shabbat is the proximity to the Kotel, where the soldiers can daven if they choose and enjoy the dancing that often ensues. The middle-aged hosts communicate with their guests in English and some Hebrew. They are originally from America and have been here for 15 years. Pamela Claman was influenced to become religious by the late, charismatic singer Shlomo Carlebach. She was on his board of directors and often traveled with him to his concerts.

And finally, an interesting word derivation: *hanpasha* – animation. Like the English word that is connected to the Latin *anima* – soul, the Hebrew *hanpasha* is connected to *nefesh* – soul. The causative structural pattern of the root *nun-peh-shin* forms the word that means "causing life," or "animation."

Warm regards, and wishes for a miraculous and illuminating Chanukah. I pray for peace here and in the world.

Wednesday, November 21, 2012

I thought some readers may be interested in my personal war siren experience. Jerusalemites heard an *az'akah* (siren) on Friday night. I locked my door and started to descend to our shelter. All the female members of my building were in the hallway and I was told that that was a safe place to stay, which we did for 10 minutes. In my neighborhood mostly men, though not exclusively, go to shul on Friday nights, while women daven at home. Shortly following the *az'akah*, 18 girls, who had stopped in nearby buildings for shelter as they walked from their seminary, came to listen to me lecture on how I raised two Orthodox rabbis and two Orthodox rebbitzens in West Lafayette, Indiana. Most were from big cities, such as New York and Baltimore, so they were interested in my subject.

However, back to the *az'akah*. The fact that I knew how to respond was not always the case. Thirty-eight years ago, on Shabbat Yom Kippur, I was resting at home after being released two days earlier from Hadassah Hospital with my 6-day-old baby, Ronit. When I heard the siren about two o'clock in the afternoon, I assumed there was a fire, since I had never experienced a war before. Also, in contrast to our recent episode when rockets have been falling on the South for days, the Yom Kippur War was a total shock. Had I thought a bit more, I would have remembered that in Jerusalem there is a law that all buildings must be made of Jerusalem stone, and so the number of major fires is fewer than that of other areas. In any event, neighbors came to my door immediately and escorted me and my baby down to the shelter. I was very glad I was nursing my newborn, so I was prepared to remain a while, if necessary. My three older children joined us soon after.

Motzaei Shabbat, December 22, 2012

Prime Minister Netanyahu reflected the feelings of so many bereaved families here who have lost children to the attacks of our neighboring enemies. With compassion and with the empathy of our nation, Netanyahu voiced his condolences to President Obama on the recent massacre that occurred in the school in Connecticut. May such an outrageous tragedy never occur again.

In December, the flagship tourist attraction here—Chamshushalayim—is the central cultural festival of the winter season. It attracts tens of thousands of visitors to the capital each year, thus attesting to the fact that Jerusalem has become an international cultural and tourist center. This is the first time I have participated in a Friday morning opera, *Masters and Servants*, a fantasy based on five of Mozart's operas. Jerusalem doesn't yet have its own opera company, but this pastiche featuring very talented singers with a 20-piece orchestra on stage was a great treat for me.

I read in *The Jerusalem Post* that just in time for Chanukah the Israel Antiquities Authority discovered some archaeological remains of a farm from the Hasmonean period, on a main street in the Jerusalem neighborhood of Kiryat Yovel—a street that leads directly to the Hadassah Medical Center. According to excavation director Daniel Ein Mor, "Little is known about the culture and history of the people of Jerusalem and the surrounding countryside in the period superseding the Maccabean revolt." Therefore, the discovery of the site will provide a lot of information about the customs of daily life in the Hasmonean period.

Another item culled from *The Jerusalem Post*: The root *zayin-mem-resh* is connected both to playing music (*tizmoret* – orchestra) and to singing (*zammar* – singer). Doubling the last consonant of the root, in this case the *resh*, is a means of creating a diminutive form. Thus *zamrir* is a short *zemer*, i.e. "a short song or tune."

Our newspapers are filled with the various political alliances between parties to ensure the desired majority in the next Knesset after the elections...so much speculation, and so many op-eds, most of which I regret to say I don't fully grasp. This is such a small country and there are 34 political parties entering the fray! Election Day is coming up in less than a month. Actually, I find it refreshing to focus on the tumultuous elections, competitive as they may be, rather than some of the dangerous confrontations that have occurred in this area.

Much to my delight, a cousin whom I barely knew came to Israel on a very unusual Birthright trip. This particular program, which began in 2009, is associated with the organization and yeshiva, Aish HaTorah, and is open to women with children under 18. It sponsored five 10-day trips this year, and the eight trips planned for next year are all sold out. My cousin had an excellent time and is eager to return in a few years for her son's bar mitzvah. She commented on how nice it was to get away from the Xmas events, and that here one can see menorahs in every window.

On the first night of Chanukah, some 100 soldiers showed up at the Clamans' home, in the Old City, for candle lighting, singing and dancing. The Clamans' enthusiasm is so contagious that many of their friends and neighbors have been happy to join them in this mitzvah. Candle lighting with soldiers has continued throughout Chanukah.

Yechiel recently returned from a four-day trip to the Negev, which included sleeping in Bedouin tents. The very fresh and tasty food cooked by their hosts was supervised by a *mashgiach*. The experience included taking camel rides and staying in a hotel in the development town of Netivot. The group rode in a glass-bottom boat on the Red Sea, and their experienced guide described a whole world that exists under the water. The youngsters took several hikes, went rappelling in a nearby mountain, and also participated in jeeping. Two highlights for Yechiel were stargazing in the very clear Negev night sky, and climbing Masada, with its spectacular view and history, to daven *Shacharit* on the mountaintop at dawn. By the way, Yechiel's group included a mix of about 90 high school graduates and nine adults.

Dovid and a friend spent a Shabbat in the Negev community of Arad. There are three buses a day direct from Jerusalem, and the journey takes about two hours. I was surprised to learn that there is a considerable religious community, utilizing at least nine shuls (six Gerer, two Sephardic and one Lubavitch). Dovid and his friend stayed with Gerer Chassidim whose rabbi told them that this is the area in which our forefathers traversed, maybe even dwelled, so hundreds of his Chassidic followers moved south. Arad has interesting archeological remnants. It is a planned and quiet city with wide streets. Homes are much less expensive than in many other areas of the country, and Arad is located about a half hour ride (15 miles) from the Dead Sea. Dovid and his friend enjoyed a Friday morning hour and a half floating in the sea.

Chapter 6

2013

Friday, January 18, 2013

When one of my readers read about Dovid Sholom's visit to Arad, she wrote that she and her husband had visited the city many years ago and recalled the beautiful scenery. They learned of the healthful aspects of the area, especially for people with breathing difficulties. Experts attributed the curative qualities of Arad to the abundant flora and fauna. The City Council then enacted a law declaring that this particular combination of flora and fauna should never be changed, since Arad, with its desert air, can also be a haven for asthmatics and others with respiratory difficulties.

Recently, Jerusalem was blessed with abundant rainfall, followed by a snowstorm. As previously mentioned, the advent of snow here is cause for great joy, and the few inches that fell brought children of all ages into the streets. In place of traffic, the roads were filled with snowmen and snowball fights, and my intrepid grandchildren declared the atmosphere carnival-like. My granddaughter Yocheved, knowing I was not venturing out, brought me the welcome panacea for cold weather: some hot homemade soup.

The following morning dawned bright and clear, and I ventured out for my usual Friday errands. I found the snow mostly melted, but unfortunately, as a result of the storm, the ground was littered with broken pine branches. Bayit VeGan's fresh mountain air reminded me of the verse from Naomi Shemer's popular song "Jerusalem of Gold": *Aveer harim tzalul ka-yayin, ve-*

rayach oranim, "the mountain air is clear as wine, with the aroma of pine trees…"

The previous night, as the snow began to fall, my grandson Dovid and his friends were returning to Jerusalem from a wedding in B'nei Brak. During the traffic congestion that ensued, the yeshiva boys exited the hired bus in which they were traveling and entertained the people in the rows of stalled cars, by singing and dancing way into the night. Only in Israel!

President Peres enjoyed Jerusalem's snow by building a snowman with his bodyguards. "Jerusalem is many colors," he said outside his residence. "In the morning she is golden; in the sunset she is bluish. But when she is white, she is so beautiful, so unifying. Whatever happens in Jerusalem is a blessing. This time it is a blessing in white."

Thursday, February 21, 2013

Israeli wines are "not just for *Kiddush* anymore," *The Jerusalem Post* proudly proclaimed. In modern times, Israel's wine industry was re-established by Baron de Rothschild. The company he founded, Carmel, is Israel's largest winery, accounting for 40 percent of its wine market. Much of Israel's land is hospitable to growing grapes, and ancient winepresses have been found in many parts of the country. Nowadays, drip irrigation, insulated tanks developed specifically for Israeli climates and agricultural know-how, allow for cultivation of many grape varieties across the country and maximize the quality of every wine.

Of the 33 million bottles of wine produced each year in Israel, the majority are kosher. Israel's red, white, sparkling and dessert wines have won gold medals and trophies in major international competitions and increasingly bring home high scores from the world's leading wine critics. *L'chayim*!

Several weeks ago, my grandson Yechiel was traveling from Bar-Ilan, where his program is based, to spend Shabbat with me in Jerusalem. The Egged bus was partway to its destination, and its passengers were all seated near the front. A woman happened to look toward the back of the bus and noticed an unattended large suitcase perched on a seat. She alerted the driver, who immediately stopped the bus and ordered all the men, women and children to exit and stand at some distance from the vehicle. Meanwhile, the driver called the police who arrived with the bomb detonation squad.

All this took some time, and since this was the last bus on Friday afternoon, the travelers were becoming tense. The bomb experts declared the *cheifetz chashud* (suspicious item) to be harmless, and the passengers cheered with joy.

However, this unexpected time-delay meant that the driver would not be able to arrive home in time for Shabbat, so he promptly turned the bus around to return to Bar-Ilan and B'nei Brak.

Yechiel was surprised that several passengers were upset because their plans for Shabbat in Jerusalem were ruined, but he was with the majority who were so grateful to be alive. Here in Israel, any potential security threat is taken seriously, and so is guarding the sanctity of Shabbat!

I recently returned from a nostalgic, safe and happy trip to Key Largo, Florida, the Bahamas and Mount Kisco, New York. The first leg of my journey included time with dear childhood friends who spend the winter months in the South. What a contrast the Key Largo sea and boat culture is from my Jerusalem neighborhood! Allow me to indulge in some reflections. Gazing and strolling through the area, I couldn't help but notice how quiet and peaceful the streets were. Most homes had a large or medium sized boat in the driveway, and although I walked around at various times of the day and evening, I never saw any children about. As you can imagine, my neighborhood, 37 miles from the sea, has no boats, but you will find a mezuzah on every doorpost, and the area is teeming with the sights and sounds of children.

Key Largo has one Reform temple while my neighborhood, as I've written earlier, contains countless Orthodox synagogues and schools. The street names in Key Largo reflect the interest in sea life there, with names such as Blue Runner, Jewfish, Kingfish, Snapper, Bass and Whitefish. In Bayit VeGan, the streets are named for great rabbis, such as HaRav Uziel, HaRav Cassuto, and HaRav Frank, to name a few.

A highlight of my Florida visit was admiring my host's lush tropical garden. The area was once under water, so the ground has large limestone deposits with traces of coral. Local fruit I sampled includes sapodilla, which looks like kiwi and tastes like dates; carambola, also known as starfruit; pomelo; coconut; loquat; and kumquat. Much of the same fruit is available in Israel, but dates, which are an Israeli staple and one of the *shiv'at haminim*, are inedible when grown in Florida. This is because Israel receives its rain in the cold winter, as opposed to Florida, which enjoys dry winters and hot and rainy summers. *Etrog* trees, on the other hand, flourish in both locales.

Following my Florida sojourn, I had a reunion with some other friends on a four-day cruise to the Bahamas. When I was a teenager back in '55, I traveled to Israel for six weeks as part of a group of Young Judaea Zionist youth leaders, under the aegis of the Jewish Agency. Eleven of us have remained in touch and have been meeting about every two years, primarily in our home locales, which include Florida, Las Vegas, Kansas City, Long Island and Lafayette, Indiana. This time we enjoyed a magnificent cruise and reveled in sharing our memories of Israel in the early days of the State.

In the summer of 1955, our journey to Israel took over a week, starting with a flight from New York to Paris. After a few days in Paris we took an overnight train to Marseille and finally boarded a ship to Haifa. As we crossed the Mediterranean on the *Artza*, we did loads of singing and Israeli folk dancing on the deck. When we finally caught our first glimpse of the Land of Israel, we all cried. Nowadays, of course, the distance from New York to Israel is traversed with a single 12-hour plane ride. Driving from Haifa to Jerusalem took four and a half hours, more than twice as long as it takes today. We found the southern city of Beer Sheva to be filled with flies and camels. There was one telephone in the entire city that could be used for international phone calls. I recall standing on line in the post office, well after midnight, waiting to call my family back in the U.S. This is particularly ironic considering that in recent years Israeli technology has contributed so much to the development of cell phones. Back then, meat was a scarce luxury and eggplant was a staple; a popular recipe book offered 70 ways to prepare this basic vegetable.

Although we were based in Jerusalem, we stayed for three days in Kibbutz HaSolelim, working the land, weeding tomato plants, and eating breakfast out in the fields. Like tourists today, we shopped in the *shuk* in Jaffa and stayed in a hotel in Tel Aviv. Back in Jerusalem, we visited the Holocaust Museum at King David's Tomb where we saw, for the first time, soap made by the accursed Nazis from the bodies of Jewish martyrs. This museum is now part of Yad Vashem, which today has a huge campus. Yitzchak Ben-Tzvi, who was then president of Israel, came to talk to us in Beit HaKerem where we were based. The sum effect of this trip increased my devotion to the nascent State of Israel and firmed my resolve to make aliyah one day.

I returned from my travels just in time for Purim. This year, we observed the Fast of Esther on Thursday, as opposed to the day before Purim, which was Shabbat. The Purim revelry also began early, with many children and some adults walking the streets in costume already on Wednesday! I was privileged to attend several lectures focusing on the Purim holiday. One stressed the importance of being happy and cited many references to the word *simcha* in the Mishnah and the Talmud, as well as the *Tanya*, a major Chabad source. Another talk contrasted the word *Megillah* – which refers to the scroll we read on Purim and has the word *le-galot*, "to reveal," as its root – with the word Esther, which comes from the root *seter*, "secret." The speaker linked these concepts with the "stuffed" foods commonly eaten (in Ashkenazic communities) on Purim, such as *holopches*, *kreplach*, and of course hamantaschen. A *freilichen* Purim to all!

Wednesday, March 13, 2013

Living in Israel means living in a caring community, as has been experienced by my grandchildren. When my granddaughter Yocheved got on a bus at the backdoor with her stroller and all, she had to go to the front of the bus to pay. Leaving the stroller in the back and carrying her son in her arms, Yocheved discovered that she was missing a couple of shekels to pay her entire fare. She only needed to travel a few stops before switching to a different line, and the bus quickly reached her destination. A young man who was alighting at the same stop paid the rest of her bus fare, with grateful thanks from Yocheved, who proceeded to the back to retrieve her stroller and then exited.

When my grandson Yechiel was traveling from Bar-Ilan to Jerusalem, which is close to an hour's journey, he realized that he only had American money in his wallet. The bus driver had one more stop to collect passengers before he would zoom off to Jerusalem; Yechiel was told he would have to get off at that stop. However, the driver announced Yechiel's dilemma on his microphone. Immediately, two yeshiva boys got up and paid his fare. He pleaded with them to take some of his U.S. dollars in exchange, but they demurred, considering their act a complete mitzvah.

My grandson Simcha was returning to Jerusalem from a community near Modi'in, about a 40-minute ride. A young man ascended the bus and discovered he didn't have enough money with him to pay his fare. He had a reservation to catch a bus from Jerusalem to Eilat and intended to get more funds from a cash machine in the Central Bus Station. Simcha very graciously paid this young man's fare, refusing any recompense when they alighted.

Pesach preparations are in full swing around here. Since coming on aliyah, I have celebrated the *chag* with my family in London, Milwaukee, and at a Kibbutz guesthouse with my daughter Shira's family. This year it will be (most of) "Pesach in Jerusalem," with the seder celebration in B'nei Brak. Incidentally, hotels run their Pesach advertisement campaigns from immediately after Sukkot, when the next biblical holiday is already on people's minds. In preparation for the *chag*, the Sanitation Department is stepping up its activities; shifts are doubled, compressors and other specialized vehicles have been added. This is truly "Operation Pesach." Throughout the city there are special containers for burning *chametz* on Erev Pesach. I noticed a bus had a sign saying "This bus has been cleaned for Pesach"!

President Obama's first presidential visit coincided with the country's Pesach arrangements. The Israeli welcoming committee provided a very warm reception. Obama's entourage included 600 people, filling the entire King David Hotel and sections of two other hotels. Five thousand Israeli police officers guarded the president. In general, his remarks were very well received.

My musical ensemble generally has one gig a month, but this past month featured one gig per week, most of which were return performances. We feel we are playing close to a professional level now! We have recently added a xylophone player, bringing us to a total of seven musicians. Our performances are gratis, but we do accept (and expect) money to cover our transportation.

There is a well-known hiking path called the Israel National Trail that crosses Israel from north to south. Beginning at Metulla, near the Lebanese border, it runs south to the Gulf of Aqaba in Eilat. It is approximately 1,000 kilometers (620 miles) long and takes an average of 45-60 days to complete. However, there is a sea to sea trail, from the Mediterranean to the Sea of Galilee (the Kinneret), that spans 77 kilometers (48 miles) and takes about three and a half days to complete. Yechiel and a friend chose the latter.

They each carried a knapsack containing four liters of water, food supplies, *tefillin*, a map, matches, insect repellent, and a sleeping bag. Yechiel returned to Jerusalem and regaled me so enthusiastically about his experience. In short, he summarized his three-and-a-half-day adventure thusly: "The views were absolutely breathtakingly awesome; I met helpful Israelis on the route; I made new friends; I walked 77 kilometers from the

Mediterranean to the Kinneret; I bonded more closely with my walking partner; I improved my body strength; I learned a lot more about Israel and why I love it so much; and I had loads of fun!"

WEDNESDAY, MAY 1, 2013

The siren is sounded and it is Yom HaZikaron, Memorial Day. Most of the people in the country stop their activity for two minutes and stand, quietly praying in memory of the fallen soldiers as well as victims of terrorist attacks and anti-Semitism. There are commemorative ceremonies in honor of the many people who sacrificed their lives so that, with G-d's help, we can live in our Land of Israel.

Yom HaZikaron segues into Yom HaAtzmaut, Israel's Independence Day. Following the evening ceremonies and fireworks, parks are filled with families picnicking and barbecuing – *al hamangal*.

En route to meeting a friend for lunch, I passed a life-size metal statue of an elderly couple sitting on a bench, one holding a book and the other a cup. The sculpture was donated in memory of all the grandparents who perished in the Holocaust. Very touching.

I have an acquaintance who volunteers for a social service organization sponsored by the Ministry of Health. He attended a bar mitzvah ceremony at the Kotel for Holocaust survivors; at age 13 they had been deprived of the opportunity to celebrate. He told me how one man thanked him, saying, "I was never sure if I was really Jewish without a bar mitzvah, and you have lifted that yoke from my shoulders." He asked one of the other elderly "bar mitzvah boys" if he would like help with putting on *tefillin*. The man replied, "I have stopped speaking to G-d since the Holocaust." The volunteer felt awkward for having broached the subject of the *tefillin* ritual to a man who had evidently lost his faith long ago. And then the man said softly, his eyes moist with tears: "Persuade me."

I recently heard that the Knesset is passing legislation to provide financial aid to Holocaust survivors living here, who suffered so much in their youth and are often poor and lonely. It is perceived as a national disgrace that the government hasn't done more to help these individuals. At the same time, the Jewish people are generous and charitable. I heard of a munificent restaurateur in Tel Aviv who prepared seder meals, which were delivered gratis to the homes of Holocaust survivor shut-ins. I was reminded of my neighbor Tzvi, almost 90 years old, who is the sole survivor of his family. As he and his wife had no children, his only relatives in the world are some cousins of his late wife's. He is now in a nursing home where I try to visit him regularly. He has many terrible experiences from the war to relate, yet he has an upbeat personality and once confided to me that having experienced the worst, he is immune to depression.

A friend who recently emigrated from America shared with me the fact that there are about 15 million Jews in the world and only about 10 percent are religious. In Israel, close to 30 percent of the Jewish population is mitzvah observant. In my neighborhood I see highly educated families, among them physicians and professors who are all strictly religious. Their *frumkeit* (commitment to observance) enriches and ennobles them.

Monday, June 17, 2013

My spoken Hebrew is quite formal, and I am not very familiar with slang terms. But one word, which I have been hearing more and more, is *sababa*. Derived from Arabic, it is used to mean "cool," "fine" or "No problem, I'll take care of it." An Israeli friend used it differently and told me "I went to my grandson's school for *yom sababa*." *Yom sababa* is a Hebrew term meaning "grandparent's day"; it is a fusion of the words *saba* (grandfather) and *savta* (grandmother). Translating the word literally would lead to *saba ba* – grandfather comes. I have yet to use the word *sababa*. But then again, I'm a *savta*, not a teenager!

Some other new and interesting words I learned are: *linchor* – an onomatopoeia meaning "to snore," and a rare word with three mems in a row – *memamesh*, which means "he is actualizing."

In the Jerusalem neighborhood of Rechavia, many streets are named after medieval biblical Torah scholars, such as Ramban and Rambam. I would often confuse these two until I learned that Ramban (Rabbi Moshe ben Nachman, known as Nachmanides) is pronounced "RamBAN," with the accent on the last syllable, while Rambam (Rabbi Moshe ben Maimon, known as Maimonides) is pronounced "RAMbam," accenting the first syllable.

Several months ago, the famed British astrophysicist Stephen Hawking was scheduled to attend an international academic conference here. His university notified the conference chair that Dr. Hawking was not well enough to come. Soon afterward, the truth came to light. The scientist was persuaded by an anti-Israel lobby to boycott the event. This infuriated many people, including the conference chair, who called Hawking's decision a "vile and disgraceful one." Hawking had visited Israel three times in the past; the last occasion was in 2006. I read that, ironically, the device the scientist uses to assist him to talk was invented in Israel. So much for boycotting Israel!

In stark contrast, Barbara Streisand is in Israel this week to perform for President Peres' 90th birthday party. Her Tel Aviv concerts have been sold out for months. In addition to these highly publicized events, Streisand is scheduled to receive an honorary doctorate in philosophy from the Hebrew University in Jerusalem. Her visit has lifted the spirits of many Israelis.

On another subject, I read in *The Jerusalem Post* about a current conservation project at the Jerusalem Biblical Zoo. Human development has put a rare blind prawn at risk of extinction. The species is found in a remarkable habitat; it lives in one chamber of an ancient Roman cistern on the north shore of Lake Kinneret. The zoo has created an artificial environment for the prawns to procreate and hopefully prevent their extinction. In the past, the Biblical Zoo has successfully bred other threatened species, such as the sand cat, the Negev tortoise and the griffon vulture. The zoo is particularly interesting to visit because each animal or bird mentioned in the Bible has a biblical quote appended to its information sign, in Hebrew, Arabic and English.

My musical ensemble has been performing mostly at senior citizens' homes or clubs, where we play for an audience of 30 to 40 people. Recently, we joined a group of Orthodox women who gather together every Rosh Chodesh. They daven on a pretty rooftop in the newly gentrified Nachlaot quarter of Jerusalem, not far from the famous Machaneh Yehudah *shuk*. The view of Jerusalem was spectacular, and the rooftop garden featured all of the *shiv'at haminim*. The women sang *Hallel*, accompanied by a small harp and violin, and then enjoyed some refreshments. My ensemble provided the entertainment. This was a younger and very responsive crowd – singing, clapping and swaying (for want of space to dance) to our music. The rousing response we received was so gratifying!

AFTERWORD

My incentive for writing "Letters from Jerusalem," which form the basis for this book, was my desire to share my enthusiasm for living in Jerusalem. I was eager to convey some general human-interest information about the city not easily available through the media. In addition, I wanted to describe my impressions of my Chareidi neighborhood. Of course, I also wrote about my travels in Israel and interviewed my teenage grandchildren about their experiences in various venues. I shared some personal projects such as compiling a book about my late husband, Dr. Edward H. Simon, and founding my musical ensemble, which has performed in many senior citizens' homes, and elsewhere. So, in a sense, the letters resemble a diary.

Writing these letters has been a labor of love. Responses from family and friends have been so encouraging and often added relevant information to my letters. I'm especially pleased that my grandchildren have requested to be included in my mailing list.

I continue to write my unique news about life here in the Holy City. From the new material, perhaps I will complete another manuscript. I hope my wider public has also enjoyed their taste of Jerusalem and will be motivated to visit and experience some adventures of their own here.

Welcome and *l'hitraot*!

CONCLUSION

My horizons have been broadened and my vistas enlarged by listening carefully to the many people I meet and by experiencing so many meaningful events, trips and occasions. As with everything in life, there are often colors and nuances that can shatter preconceived notions, and I am grateful to have been granted the opportunity to grow in small and important ways. Although I miss many who are dear to me, my life is enhanced here by living in close proximity to four generations of my family. I learn from my grandchildren whose travels, visits and advice have enriched my world.

It is my hope that I've added an additional dimension to the cluster of information in the news about life in Israel. I deeply regret the loss of my husband who, with so much talent, would have found his niche here.

Do come and visit!

ABOUT THE AUTHOR

November, 2013

    Cyrelle was very active for 45 years in the small, Jewish, academic community from which she hails. Upon making aliyah, she decided to keep in touch by sending news of Jerusalem life, to be printed in her former synagogue's bulletin. Whether Cyrelle is providing the reader with the intricate details of available local and intercity public transportation, portraying Israel's dynamic and vibrant society by way of delightful stories and reports, inspiring the reader with "Only in Israel" anecdotes, sharing her many newly learned Hebrew words, or imparting insights and wisdom about our Jewish heritage, holidays and customs, her love and passion for Israel—and particularly Jerusalem—is palpable in every phrase. Cyrelle's strong feelings of Zionism are reflected in her desire to enlighten and enrich her readers about this beautiful country of ours. She stresses a positive outlook on issues that are usually not addressed in the media. In her own words: "It's this creative energy that people do not understand, because when somebody comes and writes about Israel, he is focusing on the state of conflict, and that's not the main point."

    Approximately 100 people get Cyrelle's tantalizing epistles—many of whom are Purdue University professors—and since she has received much encouragement from her readers, she has decided to compile her "Letters" into a book. It will likely be entitled *Welcome to Jerusalem: The Adventures of a Newcomer*, and should be published, hopefully, early next year.

    I feel that Cyrelle is a special emissary for Israel, as her missives certainly ignite the spark of Zionism in her readers and promote aliyah.

Channa Shapiro
Jerusalem

November, 2013

My wife and I have known Cyrelle since we were students at Purdue University in West Layette, Indiana, USA forty years ago. Cyrelle's indefatigable Zionism and unflagging love of Israel has made an immense contribution to Israel since her Aliyah in 2007. Cyrelle fulfilled her lifelong dream of Aliyah 52 years after her first visit to Israel, despite having lost her beloved husband of fifty years, and receiving treatment for cancer, at the age of 70.

Both an accomplished musician and a gifted writer, Cyrelle leapt into life in Israel. Unwilling to merely bask in the glow of her large family, Cyrelle continued studying Hebrew, organized a musical ensemble named *Tzlilai Ha'Olam*, Music of the World, and has written a regular column to keep friends and colleagues updated with positive news from Israel.

Without fail Cyrelle has sent out her "Letter from Jerusalem" for the past 6 years to over 100 recipients around the world. Her goal is to enlighten and enrich with every letter, and she accomplishes this with witty and insightful commentary on both current events and human interest items. Cyrelle's letters are an important source of hasbara for Israel to an audience that is comprised of a spectrum of individuals from professors to students. A collection of her letters will be published in the spring of 2014 and will be entitled *Welcome to Jerusalem: The Adventures of a Newcomer*.

Cyrelle Simon arrived in Israel with the help of Nefesh b'Nefesh in 2007 with a lifetime of laurels and honors behind her. Widowed and recovering from her illness she has plunged into making Israel her home, and continued her contributions to Israel and Jewish life. Bringing smiles to the faces of the elderly through her musical ensemble around Israel, and spreading good news about Israel via her almost weekly letters, Cyrelle has impacted the artistic life of the Jewish State. She has been building Israel for 60 years and will continue to do so far into the future.

Dr. Chaim Weissman

GLOSSARY

A

A Guten Shabbos: (Have) a good Sabbath

Adar: Hebrew month in which the holiday of Purim falls; usually coincides with February-March

afarsimon: an ancient plant that was grown by the shore of the Dead Sea; persimmon

aggadah: the non-legal moral, historical, and philosophical teachings of the Talmud

Akko: the city of Acre in northern Israel

aliyah: ascent; immigration to Israel

aliyah la-Torah, aliyot la-Torah (pl.): the divisions of the weekly Torah portion; People from the congregation are called up to recite blessings before and after the sections are read aloud by the Torah reader.

Ashkenazi, Ashkenazim (pl.): a Jew whose origins are from Germany or Eastern Europe

Av: Hebrew month in which Tisha B'Av falls; usually coincides with July-August

Avinu Malkeinu: a Jewish prayer of supplication recited daily during services, from Rosh HaShanah through Yom Kippur; each line begins with these two words, which mean "our Father, our King."

Avraham Avinu: our forefather Abraham

B

Bai Mir Bist Du Shein: "To Me, You're Beautiful" – a popular Yiddish song composed in 1932

balanit, balaniyot (pl.): female *mikveh* attendant

bar mitzvah: a Jewish boy who turns 13 thereby becoming morally and ethically responsible for his actions; the accompanying religious ceremony and celebration of this event

Baruch Dayan HaEmet: Blessed is the True Judge; the Jewish blessing recited upon hearing of a death

Baruch Hashem: Blessed be The Name [of G-d]; used as "Thank G-d"

bashert (Yiddish): destiny, fate; one's divinely preordained spouse

bat mitzvah: a Jewish girl who turns 12 thereby becoming morally and ethically responsible for her actions; the accompanying celebration of this event

Beit HaMikdash: the Jewish Holy Temple in Jerusalem, first built by King Solomon

Belz: a small town in Western Ukraine, near the Polish border; A well-known song "Mayn Shtetl Belz" expresses the longing for Jewish life there.

Birkat Kohanim: traditional mass priestly blessing at the Kotel on the second day of Chol Hamo'ed Pesach and the second day of Chol Hamo'ed Sukkot

bli ayin hara: literally, without the evil eye; When one relates their own or someone else's good fortune, the audience may feel pangs of jealousy at not having what that person has, and this can cause an "evil eye" to somehow harm the good fortune. One says "*bli ayin hara*" as a prayer to G-d that the *ayin hara* not take effect.

bourekas: flaky, margarine-based pastries most often filled with cheese, potatoes, or ground beef

bracha, brachot (pl.): blessing

brit/brit mila: Jewish ritual circumcision performed on eight-day-old baby boys

C

Chabad: Chassidic sect, also known as Lubavitch, that promotes and teaches Judaism throughout the world

chag, chaggim (pl.): holiday; Jewish festival

Chag Sameach: (Have) a happy holiday; the traditional greeting among Jews before and during any holiday *challah, challot (pl.):* braided bread eaten on the Sabbath

chametz: leavened foods made from one of five types of grain and forbidden to be eaten on Passover

chamutziot: cranberries

chanukiyah, chanukiyot (pl.): Chanukah menorah

Chareidi, Chareidim (pl.): pertaining to any of several sects of ultra-Orthodox Judaism that reject modern secular culture; a person belonging to one of these groups

Chassid, Chassidim (pl.): follower of the Baal Shem Tov's teachings emphasizing religious zeal, mysticism, prayer and joy

Chassidic: pertaining to Chassidim

chatan: bridegroom

chazan, chazanim (pl.): cantor; very competent male singer of liturgical music

cheider: traditional Jewish elementary school where boys start learning the Hebrew alphabet, Torah, Mishnah and even some Gemara

chesed: acts of kindness and devotion that go beyond the requirements of duty

Cheshvan: Hebrew month in which no holidays fall; usually coincides with October-November

Chevron: the city of Hebron

chiloni, chilonim (pl.): a secular Jew

chol hamo'ed: intermediate days of the Festivals of Passover and Sukkot

Chorshat HaEucalyptus: The Eucalyptus Grove — a love song to the Kinneret region in Israel

Chumash, chumashim (pl.): the Torah in printed form, as opposed to the Torah scroll; the Five Books of Moses (from the Hebrew word for five — *chamesh*)

chuppah, chuppot (pl.): wedding canopy; Jewish wedding ceremony held under the canopy

D

daven (Yiddish): pray

divrei Torah: short, edifying and inspirational remarks based on Jewish sources

drasha: scholarly interpretation of a religious text

d'var Torah: a short inspirational speech, usually based on the weekly Torah portion and including some pertinent insights

E

Elul: Hebrew month immediately preceding Rosh HaShanah; usually coincides with August-September

etrog, etrogim (pl.): yellow citron; one of four species used in a waving ritual during the week-long Festival of Sukkot

F

freilach (Yiddish): happy, cheerful; a lively song performed at a happy event

frum (Yiddish): observant of Jewish laws

G

Gadol HaDor: great Torah sage of the generation

Galitzianer-Litvak: A Galitzianer is an Ashkenazic Jew originating from Galicia, Western Ukraine, or the southeastern corner of Poland. A Litvak is an Ashkenazic Jew originating from Lithuania or a neighboring region.

gemach, gemachim (pl.): a charity that provides interest-free loans and/or lends items to people in need

Gemara: the second part of the Talmud comprising rabbinic discussions and commentary on the Mishnah

Gerer: originating from Ger, a small town in Poland

geshmak (Yiddish): tasty, satisfying; delightful

H

Hachnasat Sefer Torah: a ceremony of welcoming a new Sefer Torah into a synagogue, accompanied by music and dancing

haftarah: a short selection from the Prophets, read on every Shabbat in the synagogue following a reading from the Torah

Haggadah, Haggadot (pl.): the text recited at the Passover seder

halachah, halachot (pl.): the collective body of biblical, Talmudic and rabbinic Jewish law; a Jewish law

halachic: pertaining to halachah

Hallel: literally, praise; a prayer consisting of Psalms 113-118 recited, as a unit, on Rosh Chodesh, Pesach, Shavuot, Sukkot, and Chanukah; Religious Zionist communities recite Hallel on Yom HaAtzmaut, and some on Yom Yerushalayim as well.

hamantasch, hamantaschen (pl.): a popular triangular Purim pastry, often made with yeast and a variety of fillings, such as poppy seed, date, prune, chocolate, and more

Har Herzl: Mount Herzl, named for Theodore Herzl; the site of Israel's national cemetery and other educational facilities; located across from the entrance to the Bayit VeGan neighborhood

Hashem: literally, The Name of G-d; the name we use when referring to G-d in everyday speech, because the name itself is too holy for such use

Havdalah: the Jewish ceremony marking the end of Shabbat or a festival

hechsher, hechsherim (pl.): a certificate, or stamp, by a rabbi or group of rabbis, qualifying items (usually food) as kosher

hillulah: literally, day of joy; commemoration of the death of a righteous man or woman

holopches: stuffed cabbage

hummus: a popular Middle Eastern dip or spread made from cooked, mashed chickpeas seasoned with olive oil, lemon juice and spices.

I

Iyar: Hebrew month in which Yom HaAtzmaut is celebrated; usually coincides with April-May

K

kallah: bride

kasha (Yiddish): buckwheat groats

kasher: make kosher

kashrut: Jewish dietary laws

kaytana, kaytanot (pl.): summer day camp, usually for children aged 3 to 9

Keren Kayemet: Jewish National Fund, supporting good ecological projects

Ketivah Va-Chatimah Tovah: blessing to be inscribed and sealed for a good year

kever: grave

kfar: village

Kiddush: the ritual blessing over wine for Shabbat and the three festivals

kippa, kippot (pl.): skull cap worn by observant men

Kislev: Hebrew month in which Chanukah falls; usually coincides with November-December

klezmorim: musicians playing Jewish, traditional, Eastern European folk music

Knesset: Israeli Parliament

kohein, kohanim (pl.): a priestly descendent of Aaron

kollel: an institution of advanced Torah studies for married men

kasher le-mehadrin: the most stringent level of kosher supervision

kreplach: round noodle dough filled with ground meat and usually served with soup on certain holidays

kvell / kvelled (Yiddish): be extraordinarily pleased, delighted

L

Lag BaOmer: a minor holiday commemorating the end of a divinely sent plague that killed Rabbi Akiva's students because they did not show proper respect to one another; the *yahrtzeit* of Rabbi Shimon Bar Yochai, leading disciple of Rabbi Akiva

landsmannschaft (German): association of compatriots

l'chayim: literally, to life! a toast made when drinking a beverage with others; an informal party celebrating an engagement

lein, leined (Yiddish): read aloud the weekly portion of the Torah in synagogue

Levi'im: Levites; descendants of the Tribe of Levi

lulav, lulavim (pl.): palm branch; one of four species used in a waving ritual during the week-long Festival of Sukkot

M

Maariv: daily evening prayer service

magidim: traditional Eastern European storytellers, often traveling from town to town, whose sermons contained religious and moral instruction, and included stories of Jewish sages

Mamilla: Jerusalem neighborhood just outside the Old City; the new mall that opened there in 2007

mashgiach, mashgichim (pl.): a Jew who supervises the kashrut status of a kosher establishment; spiritual adviser of a yeshiva

mashiach: literally, anointed one; the messiah

matanot l'evyonim: charity given to at least two needy people – one of the four main mitzvot of Purim

mechitza: partition, particularly one that is used to separate men and women during religious ceremonies

mechutan: your child's father-in-law

mechutanim: your child's in-laws

medurah, medurot (pl.): bonfire lit on Lag BaOmer

Megillah: usually refers to Megillat Esther; scroll, often of parchment, read on certain holidays; one of the 63 tractates in the Talmud

Melaveh Malkah: literally, escorting the (Shabbat) Queen; a meal eaten after *Havdalah*, with singing and storytelling, to bid a proper good-bye to the Shabbat until next Friday night

Midreshet Sde Boker: educational center, in Kibbutz Sde Boker in the South, which houses a branch of Ben Gurion University, Beer Sheva

mikveh, mikvaot (pl.): ritual purification pool

Mincha: daily afternoon prayer service

minhag, minhagim (pl.): custom

minyan, minyanim (pl.): a required quorum of ten men joining together to pray

mishloach manot: gifts of food sent to family and friends on the holiday of Purim

Mishnah: the first major written redaction of the Jewish oral laws, called the Oral Torah; consists of six orders, each containing 7-12 tractates; one of the 63 tractates

mishteh: from the Hebrew word for drink — *shtiyah*; feast; banquet; occasion for drinking

Mitnagdim: literally, opponents; term dates back to the 18th century when Ashkenazi Jews in Europe, led by the Vilna Gaon, opposed the rise and spread of Chassidic Judaism

mitzvah, mitzvot (pl.): Torah commandment; a good deed

Mo'adim LeSimcha: the greeting "Happy Holiday" given during the days of Chol HaMo'ed Pesach and Sukkot

moshav, moshavim (pl.): a cooperative agricultural or technological town, with an emphasis on community labor

N

Nachal: acronym of Noar Chalutzi Lochem (Fighting Pioneer Youth); an army program that combines military service and the establishment of new agricultural settlements

naches: pride or gratification, especially at the achievements of one's children and grandchildren

nachesdig (Yiddish): anything done by children, which gives pleasure and pride to their parents and grandparents

NCSY: National Council of Synagogue Youth, an Orthodox organization dedicated to helping Jewish teenagers develop in their Jewish identity

nigun, nigunim (pl.): wordless tune, melody

Nissan: Hebrew month in which the holiday of Pesach falls; usually coincides with March-April

O

olah: (fem.) new immigrant to Israel (masc. *oleh*; pl. *olot/olim*)

Omer: the weeks between Pesach and Shavuot, which are designated as a time of partial mourning in remembrance of the tragic death of Rabbi Akiva's 24,000 disciples who died in a plague during these weeks

Oneg Shabbat: literally, joy of Shabbat; informal Shabbat gathering of Jews that takes place Friday evening or Shabbat afternoon and usually includes singing and refreshments

P

panim chadashot: at least one man, qualified to complete a minyan, who didn't attend the wedding and therefore represents a "new face" at *Sheva Brachot* to freshen the joy and happiness of the newlyweds; (Sephardic custom requires at least two men.)

parnassa: livelihood; income

parshah: the weekly portion of the Torah read in the synagogue on Shabbat

pasuk: a biblical verse

Pesach: the spring festival commemorating the deliverance of the Jewish people from slavery and their exodus from Egypt

pidyon haben: redemption of the firstborn son; a ceremony, held 30 days after the birth of a firstborn male, wherein the father of the baby redeems his son by giving a *kohein* five silver coins

Plishtim: Philistines; a non-Semitic people who came to Palestine from the Aegean Islands in the 12th century B.C.E., inhabiting the southwestern region of ancient Canaan and remaining a rival of the people of Israel for centuries

p'tcha: jellied calves' feet, also known as *galerete*

R

rebbe: a Chassidic spiritual leader

rebbitzen: rabbi's wife

Rosh Chodesh: the day (or days) celebrating the arrival of the new Jewish month

rosh yeshiva: the head of a yeshiva

ruach: joyous spirit

S

schach: temporary sukkah covering, usually of bamboo or tree branches

Sefirat HaOmer: the mitzvah of verbally counting each of the 49 days from the second evening of Pesach – the date when an *omer*-measure of barley was offered in the Temple - until the day before an offering of wheat was brought to the Temple on Shavuot

Sephardim: Jews who originated in the Iberian Peninsula (Spain and Portugal) as well as Jews of Arabic and Persian backgrounds who follow Sephardic customs

seudah, seudot (pl.): a festive meal, usually connected to the fulfillment of a mitzvah

Shabbat Nachamu: literally, the Shabbat of Consolation; the Shabbat after Tisha B'Av that brings comfort after mourning the destruction of the two Temples in Jerusalem

Shacharit: daily morning prayer service

Shanah Tovah: (Have) a good year; the traditional greeting on or around Rosh HaShanah

Shavuot: began as a harvest festival, but also commemorates the revelation at Mount Sinai and the giving of the Torah

sheitel: wig

shekel, shekalim (pl.): the basic monetary unit in Israel; the major weight of metal mentioned in the Bible, used as a bartering material

Sheva Brachot: the seven blessings uttered under the wedding canopy; a party given each day of the week following the wedding

shidduchim: a system of matchmaking in which Jewish singles are introduced to one another

shiur, shiurim (pl.): a lesson on any Torah topic

shivah: the week-long period of formal mourning for a deceased close family member

shiv'at haminim: the seven species of fruits and grains named in the Torah as the main produce of the land of Israel — wheat; barley; grapes; figs; pomegranates; olives; and dates

shloshet yemei hagbalah: the three days immediately preceding the Festival of Shavuot; Marriage celebrations and haircuts, otherwise prohibited during most of the period between Pesach and Shavuot, are permitted during these three days.

shlug (Yiddish): hit, beat

shlugging kaparos (Yiddish): the pre-Yom Kippur custom of swinging a chicken in a circle three times above one's head while uttering a prayer asking that if we were destined to be the recipients of harsh decrees in the new year, may they be transferred to this chicken; Many use money instead of chickens and then give the sum to charity.

Shmini Atzeret: the last day of the Sukkot holiday in Israel; the eighth day of the holiday (out of nine) in the Diaspora

shmitah: sabbatical year; the seventh year of the seven-year agricultural cycle mandated by the Torah for the Land of Israel

Shoah: the Holocaust

shofar, shofrot (pl.): ram's horn sounded during the month of Elul, on Rosh HaShanah, and at the close of Yom Kippur

shuk: street market

shul (Yiddish): synagogue

Shulchan Aruch: Code of Jewish Law, the most authoritative legal code of Judaism, made up of four sections, each subdivided into many chapters and paragraphs

shvarim: one of the categories of shofar sounds blown on Rosh HaShanah – three medium, groaning-like blasts

Shvat: Hebrew month in which Tu B'Shvat falls; usually coincides with January-February

siddur, siddurim (pl.): prayer book

simcha, smachot (pl.): happiness; happy occasion

Sivan: Hebrew month in which Shavuot falls; usually coincides with May-June

siyum: a ceremonial meal celebrating the completion of any major unit of Torah study, or book of the Mishnah or Talmud

Slichot: penitential poems and prayers recited several days before Rosh HaShanah (Ashkenazic custom) or throughout the entire month before Rosh HaShanah (Sephardic custom)

sufganiyot: donuts deep-fried in oil and filled with jelly or custard, traditionally eaten on the holiday of Chanukah

sukkah, sukkot (pl.): a temporary hut in which people dwell during the Festival of Sukkot

Sussya: a small village located in the southern Chevron hills, housing some ancient archeological finds

T

Taanit Esther: The Fast of Esther, before the Purim holiday

Talmud: the major body of Jewish Oral Law, comprising the Mishnah and the Gemara

Tammuz: Hebrew month that usually coincides with June-July

Tanach: the canon of the Hebrew Bible, consisting of the Five Books of Moses, the Prophets, and the Writings – a total of 24 books

techina: a Middle Eastern dip or spread made from finely ground sesame seeds

tefillin: phylacteries

Tehillim: the Book of Psalms; individual psalms

Teverya: the city of Tiberias in the Galilee

The Three Weeks: an annual mourning period, beginning the 17th of Tammuz and ending with Tisha B'Av, during which there are various mourning-related customs

Tisha B'Av: literally, the 9th of Av; a major day of fasting and mourning for the loss of the two Temples in Jerusalem

Tishrei: Hebrew month in which the High Holidays and the Festival of Sukkot fall; usually coincides with September-October

tiyul, tiyulim (pl.): outing; hike; trip

Torah: the Five Books of Moses

truah: one of the categories of shofar sounds blown on Rosh HaShanah — nine quick wailing-like blasts in short succession

Tu B'Av: a happy day on the Jewish calendar, which served as a matchmaking day for unmarried women during the Second Temple period

Tu B'Shvat: marks the beginning of a new year for trees; a day for tree-planting ceremonies

Tu B'Shvat seder: a festive meal featuring fruits in honor of Tu B'Shvat; Somewhat like the Pesach seder, there is a structure: fruits are eaten, wine (both red and white) is drunk, and verses from the Bible are read, all in a certain order.

tzaddeket: a righteous woman

tzaddik, tzaddikim (pl.): a righteous man

tzedakah: charity

Tzfat: the city of Safed in the Galilee

U

ushpizin (Aramaic): guests; the seven "guests" we invite each night into the sukkah, starting with Abraham on the first night and ending with King David on the seventh night

V

vach nacht (Yiddish): literally, night of watching; the night before the *brit mila* of a male Jewish child, when he is in need of added spiritual protection

Y

Yad Vashem: World Center for Holocaust Research, Documentation, Education and Commemoration

Yaffo: the city of Jaffa, near Tel Aviv

yahrtzeit (Yiddish): the anniversary of someone's death

Yamim Noraim: literally, the Days of Awe; the ten days beginning with Rosh HaShanah and ending with Yom Kippur; the High Holidays

Yehuda: Judah, the fourth son of Jacob and Leah

Yerushalayim: Jerusalem

yeshiva, yeshivot (pl.): an academy of intensive Torah study

yishuv, yishuvim (pl.): general name for a town or village

Yom HaAtzmaut: Israel Independence Day

Yom HaShoah: also known as Yom HaShoah Ve-HaGevurah – Holocaust Memorial Day, commemorating the bravery of the six million Jews who were killed in the Holocaust

Yom HaZikaron: National Remembrance Day for Israel's fallen soldiers and victims of terror

Yom Tov: a Jewish festival of biblical origin

Z

Zman Simchateinu: literally, the Season of our Rejoicing; the term commonly used in Jewish prayer and literature to refer to Sukkot

www.ingramcontent.com/pod-product-compliance
Lightning Source LLC
Chambersburg PA
CBHW062243300426
44110CB00034B/1454